The Generation of Trust

Public Confidence in the U.S. Military since Vietnam

David C. King and Zachary Karabell

The AEI Press

Publisher for the American Enterprise Institute

WASHINGTON, D.C.

2003

Available in the United States from the AEI Press, c/o Publisher Resources Inc., 1274 Heil Quaker Blvd., P. O. Box 7001, La Vergne, TN 37086-7001. To order, call toll free: 1-800-937-5557. Distributed outside the United States by arrangement with Eurospan, 3 Henrietta Street, London WC2E 8LU, England.

Library of Congress Cataloging-in-Publication Data

King, David C.
    The generation of trust: public confidence in the U.S. military since Vietnam / David C. King and Zachary Karabell.
      p. cm.
    Includes bibliographical references.
    ISBN 0-8447-4188-4 (pbk.)
    1. United States—Armed Forces—Public opinion. 2. Public opinion—United States. 3. United States—History—1969–
I. Karabell, Zachary. II. Title.

UA23.K4819 2002
355'.00973'0904—dc21

2002042673

ISBN 0-8447-4188-4 (pbk.: alk. paper)

Printed in the United States of America

Contents

LIST OF FIGURES

LIST OF TABLES

Acknowledgments

This monograph was supported by the John F. Kennedy School of Government's Visions of Governance in the Twenty-first Century Project and presented in November 2001 at Princeton University's Center for the Study of Democratic Politics. A previous version was given at the Duke University workshop, Democracies, Institutions, and Political Economy. We thank participants at those workshops, including Larry Bartels, Bill Bianco, John Brehm, Damon Coletta, Peter Feaver, Paul Gronke, Marc Hetherington, John Hibbing, Richard Kohn, and Wendy Rahn. The Pew Charitable Trusts supported our research. Ari Appel, Ivan Barron, Jamal Braithwait, and Terry Pierce reviewed and commented on this monograph. We are also indebted to Katharine Canfield, Ole Holsti, Samuel Huntington, James McConville, Sean Osterhaus, William Parker, John Reppert, Brian Smith, Richard Sobel, John White, and Michael Whitlock for their input.

1

Public Trust

September 11, 2001, just as December 7, 1941, exposed deadly flaws in U.S. national defenses, and the events associated with both tragedies served to mobilize the government and citizens. In the days following the September 11 terrorist attacks on the World Trade Center and the Pentagon, public trust and confidence in the federal government soared, despite a catastrophic failure to detect and deflect the terrorist attacks. Two weeks after the terrorist attacks, 64 percent of those responding to a *Washington Post* poll said that they "trust the government in Washington to do what is right 'just about always' or 'most of the time.'"[1] In April 2000 just 30 percent of Americans showed such support. In times of military crises, citizens rally around the flag to display trust in political leaders and institutions.

That we trust the federal government in times of need is no surprise, but at least since the early 1970s, most Americans claimed not to trust the federal government most of the time. In 1994, for example, before the Monica Lewinsky scandal that tarnished President William J. Clinton's reputation, and in the midst of an economic boom, just 20 percent of Americans said that they trusted the federal government to "do the right thing" most of the time or almost always, according to University of Michigan surveys. Twenty years earlier, in 1964, 76 percent of Americans expressed such support.[2] Of course, those were in the early days of the Vietnam War, when citizens were rallying around the flag once again.[3] Trust in the federal government, and confidence in the U.S. military in particular, began slipping as the war in Vietnam expanded.[4]

1

**Figure 1-1 Citizens Who "Trust the Federal Government,"
1958–2002**

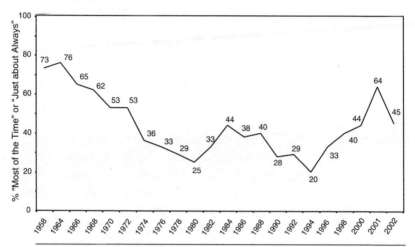

Sources: 1958–2000: National Election Studies (2000); 2001: *Washington Post* Poll (2001);
2002: CNN/*USA Today*/Gallup Polls (2002a).

The Vietnam War alone does not explain the long-term decline in trust of the federal government that happened from the 1960s through the late 1990s. Public disaffection with the war, followed closely by the Watergate scandal that brought about President Richard M. Nixon's resignation in 1974, help explain the early years of decline in public trust of the federal government, but the decline continued apace through the late 1970s. As shown in figure 1-1, trust increased during Ronald Reagan's first term in the White House before declining again from the mid-1980s through the mid-1990s. Several interesting puzzles are woven into figure 1-1, none more so than the relatively recent increase in public trust.

In some respects, then, the rally-around-the-flag effect that we have seen since September 11 is part of a longer trend. That trend is partly driven by a new generation of Americans, largely Generation X (born from 1962 through 1975) and especially Millennials (born after 1975), who trust the government, and especially the U.S. military, more deeply than their Baby Boomer parents ever have.

Our goal in this monograph is to explore the "generation" of trust in the military that has taken place since the end of the Vietnam War, because confidence in the leaders of the military is an anomaly. It has risen, gradually, just as confidence in most other institutions has declined. Our focus will be on the performance and professionalism of the U.S. military, largely since the end of the draft and the beginning of the all-volunteer force in 1974. To performance and professionalism we add "persuasion," or the careful use of advertising, movies, and the news media to portray the military's improved performance and professionalism in the best possible light.

With better military performance, improved professionalism, and calculated persuasion, the U.S. military has gained considerable trust from Americans, compared with the early days after the Vietnam War. But confidence and trust have also risen because of the impact of improved performance on a new generation of potential military recruits. As we will detail, the generation of trust is surprisingly generational. That is, how one views the performance, professionalism, and persuasion of the U.S. military depends significantly on what one read, saw, and experienced as a young adult.

If we can understand how the U.S. military gained and sustained public trust, other public institutions may be able to emulate their successes. The losses of confidence and trust go well beyond the federal government generally. (See table 1-1.) From 1971 to 2001, the percentage of Americans expressing a "great deal of confidence" in the "people running" medical institutions dropped from 61 to 32 percent. For universities the drop over the same period was from 46 to 35 percent. Even law firms, widely reviled today with just 10 percent expressing a great deal of confidence in them, saw a drop from an already low 20 percent in 1971. Other than the military, only the U.S. Postal Service and the Supreme Court increased in public esteem. With the Postal Service, perceptions of performance and professionalism were enhanced by advertising campaigns. Competing with faxes and Federal Express, the Postal Service instituted substantial internal reforms

Table 1-1 Ranking of Institutions Inspiring a "Great Deal of Confidence" in the "People Running the Institutions"

Institution	1971 %	2001 %	Change %
Medicine	61	32	−29
Universities	46	35	−11
Organized religion	27	25	−2
Major companies	27	20	−7
Military	27	44	+17
Supreme Court (1973)	23	35	+12
Executive branch	23	20	−3
Television news	22	24	+2
Law firms	20	10	−10
Wall Street	19	23	+4
Congress	19	18	−1
White House	18	21	+3
Press	18	13	−5
Organized labor	14	15	+1

Source: Harris (2001).

and improved efficiency, and advertising began in the mid-1980s. When a beautiful woman in a tight blue dress reported "two pounds, two days, two dollars," public confidence in the Postal Service went up almost overnight.

Likewise, confidence in the U.S. Supreme Court has increased, particularly as its decisions became thought of as less "political." With the abortion decision *Roe v. Wade* in 1973, the Court reached its low point in public esteem. Similarly, the Court's decision during the disputed presidential election results at the end of 2000 was widely perceived as politically motivated, and concerns were raised that the hard-won public trust would plummet. For the most part citizens have less confidence in institutions deemed "political" (like Congress and the White House) than in institutions considered nonpolitical.

Polls in 2002 showed especially strong support for the military, but we do not include them here because the General Social Survey, run out of the University of Chicago, forms the backbone of our analysis, but the survey will not be released until 2003. In the January 2002 Harris poll, however, 71 percent reported a

Figure 1-2 Confidence in Congress and the Military, 1971–2001

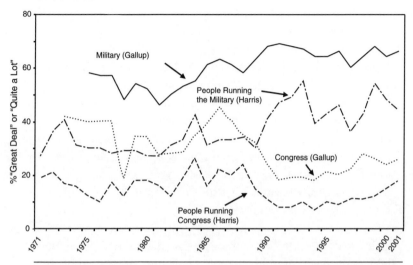

Sources: Harris (2001); "Trust in Institutions" (1998); CNN/USA *Today*/Gallup Polls (2002b).

"great deal of confidence in the military," and 50 percent said the same about the people running the White House. Those are clear rally-around-the-flag responses, born partly of the initial successes on the ground in Afghanistan. Confidence in most other U.S. institutions stayed about the same over the previous year.

Question wordings matter in surveys, and since the General Social Survey and Harris polls ask about confidence in the "people running" institutions, we should contrast that with support for the institutions themselves. The Gallup organization asks about confidence in "the military" and in "Congress." Both show higher levels of trust than when "the people running" those institutions are thrown into the mix, as shown in figure 1-2. By either measure, the military has risen in public esteem while Congress (as an institution) has declined, and regard for the "people running Congress" has been fairly flat.

The military really stands out, going from fifth on the Harris list in 1971 to number one through the 1990s. Various predictions in the mid-1980s were made regarding which institutions would maintain public confidence. In 1983 Seymour Martin Lipset and William Schneider compared public confidence among business and government groups. "Suspicion of power," they concluded,

> helps to explain why business, labor, and government have been among the lowest-rated institutions in terms of public confidence, with business usually faring somewhat better than the other two. The evidence suggests that it is the self-interested quality of business, labor, and government and the fact that they represent visible concentrations of power that turn public opinion against them. The institutions that consistently do best in confidence ratings are those most clearly identified as altruistic: science, medicine, education, religion, and the military.[5]

That prediction did not come true. Medicine, education, and religion have fallen in public esteem while the military—probably more authoritarian than altruistic—gained. The turnaround is startling, particularly since young people in general today are more antiauthoritarian than their parents and grandparents were. That is especially true of Generation X, but less true of the Millennial Generation. As Ronald Inglehart has demonstrated with public opinion surveys from around the world, the rejection of authoritarianism is strongly associated with declining support for traditional institutions.[6]

A large body of research has established that attitudes toward authority figures and authoritarian institutions tend to be firmly set during teenage years. The mid-1960s and early 1970s were a much different time for socialization from what one finds today. Throughout much of the Vietnam War, the military was widely perceived as a duplicitous, ineffective, and inefficient organization, beset by terrible racial problems, rampant drug abuse, underskilled officers and noncommissioned officers, and a general inability to adapt to the times.

Contributing mightily to the socialization of teenagers, those images were reflected in newspapers, television shows, and

Hollywood movies, which were read, seen, and absorbed by tens of millions of people. Francis Ford Coppola's 1977 film *Apocalypse Now* came complete with an insane colonel, lax discipline, and a macho commander absurdly ordering his troops to surf during an attack on a Vietcong position. The film, like *The Deer Hunter* (1978) and then the first Rambo film, *First Blood* (1982), which depicted a callous Army abandoning soldiers in Vietnam, reflected the worst cultural stereotypes of the 1970s military.

Yet twenty years later, the American military enjoys extraordinarily high levels of public confidence. Just as popular culture reflected the widespread disenchantment with the military in the 1970s, that same culture now reflects more respect and confidence. From movies such as *Top Gun* (1985) and *Saving Private Ryan* (1998) to television shows such as *Major Dad* and *J.A.G.*, the military has not enjoyed such positive portrayals since World War II. The summer 2002 VH-1 series *Military Diaries* looked and sounded like recruiting ads, but the series proved immensely popular among high school–aged viewers. And on July 4, 2002, the U.S. Army got into the video gaming industry in a big way by releasing *America's Army*. The high-end computer game was aimed at adolescents, and its preview at a May 2002 computer gaming trade show created tremendous buzz.[7]

Until the January 2002 spike to 71 percent with a "great deal of confidence" in the military after the September 11 tragedies, most of the late 1990s polling numbers for military confidence declined slightly from the highs of 1991 and 1992. After the Gulf War as much as 85 percent of those surveyed expressed a great deal or quite a lot of confidence in the leaders of the military.[8] Perhaps the Somali debacle, with dead U.S. Rangers being dragged through the streets of Mogadishu, dampened support. Perhaps the sexual harassment spotlight focused on the military after Tailhook and the Aberdeen Proving Ground affairs drained confidence, especially among women. Even factoring in that decline, however, the military today remains firmly ensconced as a vital institution that commands higher levels of public confidence than almost any other institution, governmental or other.

How then to account for the rise in public confidence of the military despite the declining trust in almost all government institutions? The military reform movement, culminating in the 1986 Goldwater-Nichols Defense Reorganization Act, played a significant role in changing the performance and professionalism of the military. Arguably, many of the successes of the nearly fifty operations since Desert Storm can be attributed to the Goldwater-Nichols Act.[9] Yet lest we look too hard at internal flowcharts, we should not overlook the potentially powerful use of persuasion targeted at young ears and eyes—ears and eyes that know the Vietnam War only as their "parents' problem."

The evolution of public attitudes toward the military over the three decades since the Vietnam War is a historical process. It forms a story of an institution pushed to the brink, of junior officers confronting failure, and of senior company grade officers instituting a series of reforms designed to reverse the military's decline. It is also a story of changes in American society, from the chaotic days of Nixon and Carter to the cheerful veneer of the Reagan years that vastly enriched the military and emphasized pride in the armed forces. It is a story of military successes in the 1980s and 1990s that were the more dramatic coming as they did in the wake of America's worst and most mortifying military defeat.

For our empirical analysis, we use the University of Chicago's General Social Survey. This is a comprehensive survey of a nationally drawn random sample of adults. The survey has used the same "military confidence" question most years since 1973.[10] Respondents (29,902 have answered the military question since 1973) reported whether they had a "great deal," "some," or "hardly any" confidence in leaders of the military.

Across the twenty-five years of those surveys, the percentage of citizens with a "great deal" of confidence in the military averages 36.44 percent. Looking at the simple percentages shown in table 1-2, support is especially high among high school dropouts (44.60 percent), political conservatives (44.44 percent), children of the Baby Boom generation, people with family

Table 1-2 Demographics and Confidence in the Military

Respondent	% "Great Deal of Confidence in People Running the Military"	Difference
Full sample, 1973–2000	36.44	na
Some high school education	44.60	
College graduate	25.51	19.09
Self-described conservative	44.44	
Liberal	30.40	14.04
Watch 6+ hours TV daily	39.59	
Does not watch TV	28.54	11.05
Millennial Generation	42.66	
Baby Boomers	31.75	10.91
Income bottom quarter	40.93	
Income top quarter	31.90	9.03
White	36.92	
Black	31.89	5.03
Male	39.49	
Female	33.99	5.50
Religious fundamentalist	39.77	
Not fundamentalist	35.02	4.75
Veteran	38.10	
Nonveteran	34.89	3.21

Note: N = 29,902.
Source: General Social Surveys Cumulative Surveys, 1973–2000.

incomes in the bottom quarter (40.93 percent), religious fundamentalists (39.77 percent), and people who watch a lot of television (39.59 percent).

By themselves, those percentages could deceive us, because many of the respondent characteristics are highly correlated. For example, religious fundamentalists are more likely to be political conservatives. People who watch a lot of television are more likely to have lower incomes and to be less well educated. Self-described conservatives are more likely to have higher incomes, and so forth. To account for how those variables related to each other, we include an appendix with a multivariate model of support for the military.

Except for the impact of having been a veteran, the basic relation-ships in table 1-2 hold up under rigorous statistical treatments.

Several of the contrasts in table 1-2 are striking. High school dropouts are almost twice as likely to express a great deal of con-fidence in the military than are college graduates. Does that mean that college graduates "know" something that high school dropouts do not? Is the skepticism of college graduates part of a more pervasive cynicism that we find within the educated elite?

Not surprisingly, conservatives have far more confidence in the military than do liberals, with a spread between them of fourteen percentage points. Conservatives in the sample tend to be wealth-ier than liberals, but higher-income Americans tend to trust the military much less than citizens with incomes in the bottom quar-ter. Clearly, something "multivariate" is going on, as we report in the appendix. Other oddities include the fact that black Americans have less confidence in the military, yet over most of the past twenty-five years, they have been more willing to enlist than any other racial group. Of particular significance for us, the so-called Millennial generation trusts the military much more than do their Baby Boomer parents (born from 1946 through 1961). That is one finding that gets stronger and stronger on closer examination. The generation (creation) of trust seems tied to the attitudes of the "X" and "Millennial" generations. We focus much more closely on the two meanings of the word *generation* in chap-ter 2. Here, we discuss a few of the findings from the General Social Surveys that hold up well to multivariate techniques, as reported in the appendix.

Multivariate techniques (in this case an "ordered probit") help us control for how a respondent's characteristics might interact. For example, young people trust the military more, but they also watch a lot more television. So what is driving the result—their age, their viewing habits, or both? The answer is clear: both mat-ter a lot, but even old folks who watch a lot of television are more likely to have confidence in the military when we hold everything else in the models constant. Younger people are slightly more likely to watch television than are the middle-aged.

That an 11.05 percent gap in confidence exists between heavy television viewers (10.5 percent of the sample) and those who watch no television (4.7 percent of the sample) may reflect the direct impact of military advertisements on public perceptions. But one's hours of television watched are positively correlated with the consumption of other entertainment.[11] People who watch a lot of television are far more likely to go to action-oriented films in movie theaters. Heavy television viewers, therefore, are more likely to see a movie like *Saving Private Ryan*. Accordingly, television viewing reflects action-oriented media consumption more generally.

With sophisticated techniques that "held constant" other characteristics of the respondents, we also found that:

- Blacks have less confidence in the military than otherwise identical whites (and blacks' confidence has not grown with racial integration).
- Women have less confidence in the military than do males.
- The better educated a person is, the less confidence one has in the military.
- Married people have more confidence in the military, although that is likely a function of *not* being single or divorced, as married respondents tend to be more confident about most institutions.
- One's veteran's status does not hold up to multivariate tests, except for Vietnam War veterans, who are much less likely to have confidence in the military. Indeed, Vietnam veterans have the lowest confidence in the military of any subset of Baby Boomers.
- As expected, the more politically conservative a respondent is, the more confidence one has in the military. We find no evidence that conservatives' confidence in the military has strengthened as the military's officers have themselves become more conservative.
- Strong ideologues are more likely to be extremists, and they are represented in the model if their self-reported ideologies were "very liberal" or "very conservative." Ideological extremists

at both ends of the spectrum—if we hold all else equal—express less confidence in the military. The far Right (the black helicopter crowd) and the far Left (the no helicopters crowd) are strange bedfellows, but they share certain skepticism of the U.S. military.

- Religious fundamentalists are more confident of the military, but we doubt that this is driven by religious doctrine or even shared conservatism (since that is controlled in the model). Rather, we use religious fundamentalism as a rough proxy for acceptance of or tolerance of discipline and traditionalism. Seen that way, respondents who are more accepting of traditionalism are also more likely to trust the military.[12]
- In years when there are large public failures (such as the failed 1980 Iranian hostage rescue), public confidence falls.
- Military successes (like the 1994 intervention in Haiti) help to boost confidence.

Our most striking findings, though, surround the strong generational influence in how one sees the U.S. military. Generation Xers and Millennials are far more likely than their Baby Boomer parents to have confidence in the military. Indeed, the distaste that Baby Boomers had thirty years ago still seems to have a strong influence on how they view the military today—despite the military's increased performance, its improved professionalism, and the public persuasion campaigns that have transformed Hollywood. What is going on?

2

The Generational Gulf

Two gulf wars raged in 1991. In Kuwait and Iraq, U.S. and coalition troops pushed Saddam Hussein's Revolutionary Guard deep into Iraqi territory. The hundred-hour war seemed to lay the ghosts of the previous generation's war to rest. Troops returning home were met with parades and patriotism. Confidence in the U.S. military ran high, polling the biggest numbers since Vietnam.

Yet in living rooms across America, a second gulf war continued long after the troops had returned from the Middle East. Parents who came of age during the Vietnam War were, for the most part, lukewarm about the military. But their children had very different views. Unlike their 1960s-era parents, they hungrily embraced the military as a symbol of America's technical and moral superiority.

During the weeks of the air war, millions of young people sat in front of their televisions and watched in rapt attention as graphics of "smart bombs" and exploding bunkers showed the progress of the American bombing campaign. That was certainly the case in one South Boston home, where fourteen-year-old Andrew Lee absorbed the television coverage much the same way he would have experienced a video game, except that this video-game war came complete with missile-mounted cameras showing the action. Three years later, wrote Tom Ricks, "high-strung Andrew Lee" joined the Marines. "Then he caught a bus back to South Boston and told his parents. His mother, a social worker in a Boston school, was distraught. For months she tried to talk him out of it. 'My mother, there's a real generation gap between she and I,' Lee [would] later explain. 'She's a good woman and an excellent mother, but she comes out of the Vietnam thing.'"[1]

Or take the case of young Paul Kopacz. A troubled teen, he was mentored by the fathers of friends. One of those friends took Paul to see the film *Top Gun*. It proved to be a pivotal moment in his life. Finally, he found something he desperately wanted to do. "While he was in high school, Operation Desert Storm was launched. Paul didn't want to miss the experience and tried to enlist, but his mother wouldn't sign."[2] Determined, Kopacz made his way into the Citadel, then on to Quantico, Virginia. Now, over his mother's objections, Lieutenant Paul Kopacz is living out his own *Top Gun* dreams.

Young people in America today have a genuinely positive view of the U.S. military. In late 1998, for example, 52 percent of the nineteen- and twenty-year-olds surveyed by the University of Chicago's General Social Survey said that they had a "great deal of confidence" in the "people running the U.S. military."[3] But the figures for the total population were lower. Thirty-six percent of the general public reported a "great deal of confidence," and the lowest support came from people who were teenagers in the mid- to late 1960s. When it comes to trust in the military, a gulf divides the generations.[4]

This is not the first time a generational gulf has emerged. At the dawn of World War II, thousands of young men dropped out of high school and clamored to enlist in the weeks after Pearl Harbor. Twenty-five years later as the Vietnam deployment began in earnest, young people had an equally vehement reaction, but then it was against the military. Draftees seeking student defer-ments inundated colleges and universities.

Where one divides generations is arbitrary, though pivotal events—the Great Depression and the Vietnam War—are impor-tant in socializing and binding large groups. (See table 2-1.) Our understanding of generational dynamics is heavily influenced by William Strauss and Neil Howe, but a number of others have recently noted that children born since the mid-1970s (these are *not* Gen Xers) behave in distinct ways. They are more spiritual,[5] more likely to become involved in community service,[6] and more likely to be fiscally conservative while embracing socially liberal

Table 2-1 Generation Birth Ranges

Generation	Born after	Born before	Key Socializing Events
Depression		1930	Roaring '20s, Great Depression
War	1929	1946	World War II, Korean War
Baby Boom	1945	1962	Vietnam War, civil rights, Watergate
X	1961	1976	Economic stagnation, Gulf War
Millennial	1975		Internet revolution, September 11 attacks

programs. They grew up with the Internet being a pervasive part of their lives.

In *Millennials Rising,* Neil Howe and William Strauss describe an engaged and civically active generation just beginning to make its mark on the world as its oldest members graduate from college. A recent poll by the Institute of Politics at Harvard University confirms Strauss and Howe's predictions showing extremely high rates of participation in community service and concern for issues involving the community and the nation. That survey, done in October 2001, presented the first look at the generation whose lives will be indelibly marked by the events of September 11.[7]

Strong rally-around-the-flag tendencies are clearly evident, with a whopping 93 percent of college undergraduates claiming to be patriotic Americans, with "very patriotic" the largest response category at 49 percent. But despite predictions to the contrary, patriotism does not necessarily translate into a rush to join the military in the fight against terrorism. Only 15 percent said that they were likely to volunteer for military service or enroll in a Reserve Officers' Training Corps program. Likewise, a mere 17 percent said that they were seriously considering a career in the military. On the demand side, military recruiters reported a doubling or tripling of contacts and inquiries in the days following

September 11. That did not result in higher enlistment rates, because the military had a limited number of openings. The enthusiasm from young people did, however, improve the average test scores and educational backgrounds of the post–September 11 recruits. Perhaps the Internet generation is not ready to give up the tremendous wealth promised by the new economy; the highest response returns for a future profession went to a career in business.

Yet despite that unwillingness to serve voluntarily in the nation's military, poll respondents are surprisingly comfortable with the idea of a military draft. A total of 31 percent claimed that they (strongly or somewhat) supported reinstating the military draft, and 29 percent said that if the draft were reinstated, they would eagerly serve. University of Tennessee at Chattanooga student Zach Smith exclaimed, "I'd be happy to go to the draft now."[8] That leaves a majority willing to serve their country through a draft system. Most strikingly, that suggests an end to perceptions associated with the draft in the wake of the Vietnam War. We take that less as an indication of dissatisfaction with the all-volunteer force; rather, it seems to be a sign that the Millennials trust the military to use responsibly the manpower they would provide in the event of a draft. Nobody likes the idea of being forced into something, but if there were no choice in the matter, perhaps serving in a highly successful and professional military does not sound like such a bad deal after all.

It is important to remember that the Institute of Politics poll is limited to college students. It provides a nice window into the minds of young people in the wake of September 11, but it does not tell the whole story. Many young people, especially those who consider military service, are not in college. More data are necessary before we can generalize to the whole population. It is possible that young people who are not in college have very different views about the military and society in general. As shown in the General Social Survey data in chapter 1, a college education is the single best predictor for lowering confidence in the military. Trust in the military among noncollege Millennials is most likely even higher than we found in the Harvard survey.

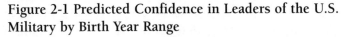

Figure 2-1 Predicted Confidence in Leaders of the U.S. Military by Birth Year Range

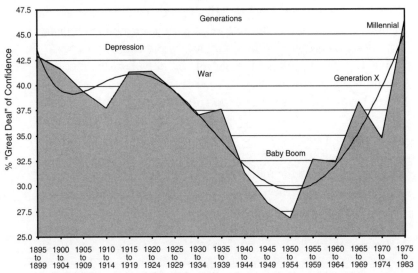

Source: Predictions from ordered probit models using General Social Surveys (1973–2000).

How strongly do the events of one's generation shape how the armed forces are viewed? To make the generational distinctions less arbitrary, we ran the ordered probit shown in the appendix with fixed effects for every year of the survey. Then, we used the model to predict the support level based on birthdays. That approach allows us to see the predicted confidence in the military by birth year, with everything else in the model held constant.

Figure 2-1 pools the predicted responses from a model that includes data drawn over twenty-five years. The dip in confidence for people who came to age during the Vietnam War is unmistakable. Controlling for everything else—race, gender, education, and so on—someone born in 1952 has the lowest predicted level of confidence in our military today. Young adults born since 1974 have the highest level of predicted confidence in the military. The connection to successes in the Gulf War, on the battlefield, and on television seems clear.

The surge in support for the U.S. military has taken many observers by surprise, coming as it did at the tail end of Generation X. A generation often labeled "selfish" and "cynical" and unambiguously distrusting of authority has embraced the U.S. military. Or at least the generation has embraced the image of the military that it came to expect in the age of the all-volunteer force and recruitment advertisements.

We have good reasons to expect that the next generation, the Millennials, will continue to support the military, at least to the extent that the military is seen as a home for national service. The Millennials, who were born after 1975 and began graduating from high school in the mid-1990s, display a commitment to community service and the public arena unlike any other since the World War II generation, born between 1901 and 1929.[9]

Until the September 11 tragedies, all of that enthusiasm, however, had not solved the military's recruitment problems. Although today's young people are more confident about the U.S. military than their parents were, on average, that has not translated into an increased willingness to join the armed forces. In a 1983 survey of high school seniors, 17.5 percent said that they "want to serve in the armed forces." By 1994, when Andrew Lee graduated from South Boston High School, the percentage dropped to 11.8. In 1997 that number stood at 12.9 percent of high school seniors.[10]

In short, a disconnect exists between the generally positive view that young people have of the military and their enlistment rates. In fiscal year 1999, for example, the U.S. Army sought to recruit 74,500, but fell short by 6,291 young men and women. Likewise, the Air Force fell 1,727 short of its goal of 34,400.[11] The U.S. Navy and Marine Corps, on the other hand, both exceeded their enlistment goals for 1999—results due partly to bonuses paid enlistees and to deft advertising. All of that turned for the better in fiscal year 2000, and every branch of the military had to turn away potential recruits. (See table 2-2.) It is important to note that the turnaround happened before the September 11 tragedies, and it seems closely correlated with Pentagon advertising budgets.

Table 2-2 Recruitment Success Rates, Fiscal Year 2000

Service	FY 2000 Goal	Actual FY 2000 Recruits	Percentage of Goal Accomplished
Army	80,000	80,100	100
Navy	55,000	55,100	100
Marine Corps	32,400	32,400	100
Air Force	34,000	35,200	104
Total	201,400	202,800	100

Source: Cohen (2001, 167).

Advertising budgets for all branches of the military mushroomed in fiscal year 2000, and even as the economy remained strong, recruitment goals were met by all the active branches and also, as a group, the reserve forces. Before 2000, advertising buys were usually made for national broadcasts, and many of the advertising purchases did not reflect what kinds of shows were being watched by the target audiences. So instead of extensive advertising on, for example, *Monday Night Football,* the services designed more up-to-date messages for television and for programs on the WB Network, with programs that typically draw a younger demographic.

We will return to that recruitment conundrum, but regardless of the enlistment rates, confidence in the U.S. military by children of the Baby Boomer generation remains strong. What did the military do that helped boost confidence, especially among the youngest Americans? Since the closing days of Vietnam, the military's performance, professionalism, and persuasion proved key.

3

Performance

In January 1968 nearly a half million American soldiers were stationed in Vietnam. President Lyndon B. Johnson was determined to prevent forces loyal to Ho Chi Minh from overthrowing the pro-Western government of South Vietnam. In August 1964 the U.S. Congress authorized the president to use substantial forces to protect South Vietnam. In the summer of 1965, Congress approved the dispatch of several hundred thousand combat troops. Over the next three years, the number of U.S. troops stationed in Vietnam increased, and more young American men were drafted. All along, the U.S. government and the leaders of the military assured the American public that the war against the Vietcong and the communist troops in North Vietnam was being won—and won decisively. After years of such assurances, the North Vietnamese staged a multipronged surprise attack on American and South Vietnamese positions throughout the South in January 1968. Eventually rebuffed, those attacks, which occurred during the Vietnamese New Year holiday known as Tet, came as a sudden, dreadful shock. The illusion of U.S. military might was shattered.

The Tet offensive was a propaganda victory for North Vietnam. That was, in fact, the primary point. The Vietcong and North Vietnamese commanders might have hoped for victory on the battlefield, but they understood the importance of symbols. They knew that official spokesmen for the U.S. government routinely underestimated their strength, and they knew that the war was generating student unrest. The Tet offensive involved more than 80,000 North Vietnamese soldiers in conjunction with the

Vietcong. They launched a simultaneous assault on dozens of targets throughout South Vietnam. They attacked the six largest cities, including the imperial capital of Hue and the U.S. embassy in Saigon. The intensity and organization of the attack took American military commanders by surprise, but they quickly adjusted and soon turned back the offensive on every front.[1]

The damage, though, had been done—not to the American or South Vietnamese military, but back home in the United States to the American public's perception of the war. Having listened to the assurances of President Johnson, of Secretary of Defense Robert McNamara, and of General William Westmoreland, the public tended to believe that up until January 1968 the war effort had been showing slow but steady progress. Right or wrong, the press and the public interpreted the Tet offensive as a resounding military defeat. It was portrayed in the most negative light possible by an American press corps that was deeply suspicious of the "official line." The Tet offensive may have been a military bust for the North Vietnamese, but the public saw the offensive as proof that military officers and civilian officials had been lying to them.[2]

The Vietnam War was a watershed for public attitudes about government. Mass protests against the Johnson and Nixon administrations demonstrated the depth of public disenchantment with the war and with the officials responsible for waging it.

Opinion polls reflected the sharp drop in public confidence with government in general, and they showed a particularly dramatic decline in confidence in the military. In short, after 1968 public confidence in the military was deeply shaken.[3] In a National Opinion Research Center survey taken in 1973, for instance, only 32 percent of respondents said that they had a great deal of confidence in the people running the military.[4] Sixteen percent reported having hardly any confidence at all in the military leaders. The corresponding numbers for Congress in that year were even worse, with 24 percent saying that they had a great deal of confidence, 59 percent saying some, and 15 percent saying hardly any. In 1974, with the Watergate hearings being nationally televised, only 14 percent of respondents said that they had a great deal of confidence in the people running the executive branch. Gallup poll numbers reflected similar trends. By way of comparison, people in those years expressed significantly greater confidence in institutions such as universities, the medical profession, and even public schools and television: places where, through 1968, the public's faith had not yet been shaken by events similar to the rude awakening of the Tet offensive.[5]

From the rubble of the Vietnam War, a new army would rise, but between 1968 and 1975 the picture was grim. Few in the military would have predicted that by the late 1980s they would once again be held in high public esteem. While the crisis in public confidence was evident, the crisis in self-confidence that afflicted officers and enlisted men was even more striking.[6]

In those years military officers weaned on images of patriotic Americans warmly greeting their warriors returning from combat abroad found themselves reviled as warmongers in an unjust conflict. Resistance to the draft increased as the war dragged on, and after 1968 political leaders began to distance themselves from the war rhetorically. Between 1969 and 1972, however, thousands of Americans were still losing their lives in Vietnam, even as Nixon gradually withdrew American troops. Responding to a sharp shift in public opinion after the Tet offensive, political leaders gave up on the war. Officers watched as newspapers were saturated with coverage of abuses such as the massacre at My Lai, and they grew wary and disillusioned as their own troops deserted or attempted to kill their officers. Between 1965 and 1971 the desertion rate increased by nearly 500 percent. The Defense Department estimated that from 1969 to 1972 there were nearly 800 "fraggings," incidents in which officers were killed by their enlisted men.[7] In the face of those realities, military morale plummeted.

"For midlevel officers," commented retired Air Force General John Shaud, "Vietnam was an indelible experience." The public perception was that the military had lost the Vietnam War, and officers and noncommissioned officers were resigning their commissions in droves. The nadir was the evacuation of the U.S. embassy in Saigon in 1975. According to Major Jim Kean, who was stationed at the embassy, "The whole world was coming apart. Ten years of effort. $140 billion. All the promised commitments. Some people, it just undid them."[8]

A mix of enlisted and drafted personnel carried out the evacuation of Saigon. In 1970 the President's Commission on an All-Volunteer Armed Force recommended that the draft be phased out and that the military turn purely to volunteers to fill its ranks. In 1973 the draft was abolished, and in 1974 the all-volunteer force came into being. Although in time the all-volunteer force would remake the military for the better, initially it was a disaster. Young officers in particular viewed the all-volunteer force as a betrayal of the concept of national service. Faced with predictions that the new volunteer army would lead to racial imbalances and underskilled soldiers, many of those young officers bitterly resigned their commissions. During the 1970s, the fears that led to the resignations seemed more than justified.

The Marine Corps, for instance, discovered that many of its volunteers had joined the corps primarily for the purpose of avoiding the Army, which had the worst reputation of the services in the wake of the Vietnam War. At one point, fewer than half of Marines were high school graduates. "Many ill-adjusted, antisocial young men ended up in our ranks," commented then–Brigadier General Bernard Trainor in 1978.[9] Violence and crime at armed forces recruit depots were recurrent problems, and court-martials, desertions, and incidents of soldiers away without official leave were at all-time highs.[10] Recruiting quotas could not be met, and by 1979 the Army alone fell 17,100 soldiers below its recruitment quota of 159,200, with more than a third of its recruits high school dropouts. Within the entire military in 1980, more than a quarter of soldiers admitted that they had recently or regularly used illegal drugs. The depth of the problem was succinctly expressed by the Army chief of staff, General Edward (Shy) Meyer, who said in his testimony to Congress early in 1980, "Basically what we have is a hollow Army."[11]

The lowest point of the "hollow" era came in April 1980. After heated debate within the administration, President Carter authorized an attempted rescue mission for the hostages being held in the U.S. embassy in Tehran. The mission, called Desert One, failed. A helicopter collided with a C-130 refueling aircraft, and eight crew members died. Coming amid a long hostage crisis and after the Soviet invasion of Afghanistan in December 1979, Desert One seemed to signify that the United States was a dispirited nation incapable of protecting even the lives of American officials abroad. While Desert One was, in fact, a highly ambitious, complex, and risky operation, the press portrayed it as a pathetic effort by a weak president and a hollow military, and that impression stuck.[12]

When the highest-ranking officer in the Army referred to the corps as "hollow," with public confidence decreasing and with a pervasive sense that the all-volunteer force had been a terrible miscalculation, military morale plummeted. The loss in Vietnam and the internal problems of the institution left the military in a state of near crisis. The challenge for the military was to find ways to reform internally and to mend the damage of the Vietnam War.

Coming Out of the Shadow: Military Reform and Success

Within the 1980s, military morale was slowly improving. Budgets rose, first in 1980 under Carter and a Democratic Congress and then continually under Reagan and a Republican Senate. The so-called Reagan buildup actually began in Carter's last year, in response to the Iranian revolution and the Soviet invasion of Afghanistan. Carter, however, exhibited little enthusiasm for that remilitarization, even though he had been a career Navy officer as a young man. It took a former actor, who had played military men on film, to reinvigorate the military.

The Reagan buildup and tax cuts generated high budget deficits, but from the military's perspective, they were a definite good. Observed General John Shaud, "The Reagan effect gave us the funds to sustain readiness and to innovate for future conflicts. The positive effect on morale can't be overstated."[13]

Reagan was also a strong supporter of the military and of values that resonated with the traditional military code of honor, courage, and commitment. He spoke glowingly of the armed forces, and soldiers received his brand of patriotism as a welcome relief after years of public vilification and neglect.[14]

In addition, the post–Vietnam War years of internal upheaval and work within the military began to show results. "We stuck to the standards that made us the best fighting force the world has ever known," reflected one junior officer years later. "We got back to basics. We stressed hard realistic training and core values. We held seminars on what went wrong in Vietnam."[15] After years of violence and racial incidents at bases both at home and abroad, the all-volunteer force started to cohere. With the larger budgets came pay raises for both commissioned and noncommissioned officers, and with better pay, the armed forces became a more appealing profession for high school graduates. Thanks to a reformed version of the GI Bill, enlisted soldiers had the promise of money for college at the end of their enlistment period, and that made the military more attractive. During the late 1970s, the United States began the arduous process of shifting away from an economy based on heavy industry and toward an economy based on information and services, which required college-educated workers. Then, enlisting in the military became a way to prepare for a career in the changing economy of the 1980s. Although the military in those years still suffered from the legacy of the Vietnam War, it gradually started to emerge from its ten-year aftershock.

Internal Military Reform. The military reform movement, begun in Congress and viewed skeptically by many in the Pentagon, eventually played a critical role in internal morale and external confidence. In the mid-1970s and early 1980s, Senators Gary Hart and Robert Taft, Jr., and senior staffer Bill Lind began working on legislation to overhaul the military's internal structures. More broad-reaching still, the reform movement challenged the military's traditional attrition approach to warfare.[16]

Fearful that the Army in particular had not learned the right lessons from the Vietnam debacle, military reformers began a lively debate about military strategy. In 1976, for example, the Army released its new tactical doctrine, called the "active defense." Lind countered with a lengthy critique. Active defense, he argued, reflected attrition warfare based on mutual casualty-inflicting contests like the First World War Battle of Verdun and the battles of Vietnam. Lind believed that the new doctrine was 180 degrees wrong. Instead, Lind argued that tactics should reflect maneuver warfare like the German blitzkrieg, whose surprise and rapid movement shattered the enemy's ability to fight effectively. Attrition versus maneuver warfare became the central debate in the reform movement of the late 1970s.

By the mid-1980s, the armed forces responded to the debate by retooling their war colleges and postgraduate education programs to highlight lessons learned from the Vietnam War. Central to the new approach was Colonel Harry Summers's 1982 book *On Strategy: A Critical Analysis of the Vietnam War.* Colonel Summers argued that the U.S. Vietnam strategy violated most, if not all, of the principles in Carl von Clausewitz's *On War.* Summers's central thesis was that a "lack of appreciation of military theory and military strategy (especially the relationship between military strategy and national policy) led to a faulty definition of the nature of the [Vietnam] war."[17] Eventually, both the Army and the Marine Corps officially shifted their war-fighting doctrine from attrition to maneuver, and the military reform movement culminated in the 1986 Goldwater-Nichols Defense Reorganization Act.

Among other things, the act dramatically altered the role of the chairman of the Joint Chiefs of Staff. The law transformed the chairman of the Joint Chiefs into the principal military adviser to both the president and the secretary of defense. It also placed the service chiefs beneath the chairman in the chain of command.

The full import of those changes became evident several years later. In 1989 General Colin Powell assumed the duties of the chairman of the Joint Chiefs. Powell promptly asserted his authority over the service chiefs and began to give shape to what became known as "the Powell Doctrine." An outgrowth of the philosophy of former secretary of defense Casper Weinberger, the Powell Doctrine dictated that any military use of force should involve overwhelming numbers, clear goals, and a high probability of success. That approach has dictated most subsequent American military operations.[18]

Success on the Battlefield. After humiliations in Iran and Beirut, the remainder of the 1980s was a time of almost unbroken military successes. In October 1983 President Reagan ordered the invasion of the Caribbean island of Grenada. Dubbed operation "Urgent Fury," the Grenada invasion was the largest use of force since the end of the Vietnam War. It involved more than 6,000 men, who staged an amphibious landing on an island garrisoned by approximately 3,000 Cuban and Grenadian soldiers. Although coordination problems plagued U.S. forces, the island was taken within days, and the American public registered high levels of support for the invasion of an island few of them had ever heard of.[19]

In December 1989 President George H. W. Bush authorized a far larger operation, targeting Manuel Noriega and the Panamanian Defense Forces. Operation "Just Cause," led by General Maxwell Thurman, oversaw 24,000 U.S. troops occupying the Panama Canal Zone and Panama City in fewer than five days. That success was capped by the rapid capture of Noriega. The invasion, which seemed to violate most standards of international law, resulted in only muted international outcry. The reaction in the United States was generally positive. In the months leading up to the invasion, Noriega had been effectively demonized in the media as the archetype of an evil, corrupt drug lord. As a result, few Americans gave the legitimacy of the invasion deep consideration. Other factors only added to the impression that the invasion was a just act of apprehending a criminal rather than an invasion of a sovereign country. Noriega had few friends in Latin America, and the other Latin American states did not exactly rush to his defense. Even more, the professionalism of the American armed forces strongly contrasted with the thuggish appearance of Noriega and his Dignity Battalions.[20]

The Panama invasion was overshadowed by the collapse of communist governments in Eastern Europe, followed by the rapid collapse of the Soviet Union. The defeat of the Soviet Union in the cold war was interpreted by many as a tremendous military victory for the United States. The dismantling of the Warsaw Pact and the disintegration of the Soviet Union in 1991 ended four and a half decades of military tensions between the two world superpowers. The Reagan buildup in the 1980s brought military personnel and equipment to such high levels that the Soviet Union could no longer keep up. On December 25, 1991, the U.S.S.R. formally disbanded, ending one of the most intense conflicts in history.[21] The power of the military was one of the key factors that had allowed the United States to contain the spread of communism for nearly half a century. At the end of that conflict, the U.S. armed forces emerged undisputedly as the most powerful military in the world.

Then came the Gulf War. In August 1990 President Bush authorized "Desert Shield," the American military buildup in Saudi Arabia. After heated debate within the United States and the United Nations, Desert Shield became "Desert Storm" on January 15, 1991. Although public opinion about a potential war with Iraq was split as of early January, once the bombing began, the American public rallied around the flag and swung behind the war.[22] While untold thousands of Iraqis died during the bombing, for a generation of Americans the Gulf War seen nightly on television was a spectator sport, not unlike football or baseball. The team wore red, white, and blue.[23]

At first, the Gulf War did not seem like such a watershed in public confidence in the military. True, President Bush talked of laying the Vietnam War syndrome to rest once and for all. But the initial public support for the president and the troops was typical of the public reaction to most wars. It quickly became clear that the Gulf War was a break from the past and that the shadow of the Vietnam War was finally lifting.

The Korean War and the Vietnam War had tested the strength and staying power of the rally-around-the-flag instinct. The Vietnam War demonstrated that if large numbers of American soldiers were killed in a conflict whose goals were murky and whose time frame was drawn out, the public would eventually turn against the war. During the Gulf War, U.S. military and civilian leaders had the precedent of the Vietnam War very much in their minds. With the soul-searching of the late 1970s and the move away from set engagements that had characterized the military reform movement, Army and Air Force leaders, along with the White House, were determined to avoid a repetition of the Vietnam War by setting clear goals and basing strategy on a rapid strike.[24]

In that objective they succeeded brilliantly. While the Gulf War left Saddam Hussein in power in Iraq, his army was ejected from Kuwait, his military strength was significantly diminished, and American approval for the performance of the president and the military reached record highs. At last, blared countless newspapers, magazines, and even Bush himself, the United States could move beyond the legacy of the Vietnam War.[25] Nearly 90 percent of the American public expressed a great deal of confidence in the military; more young men and women volunteered for service; Colin Powell and General Norman Schwarzkopf were revered as national heroes; and soldiers returning from the gulf were greeted by throngs of people waving flags and showering them with affection and confetti.

The success in the gulf was followed by a setback on the Horn of Africa. The sense of invincibility gained from those tickertape parades may have played a role in the ill-fated decision by President Bush to send American forces to Somalia at the end of 1992. Ostensibly dispatched to end the famine and restore order to the capital, Mogadishu, the mission of the 25,000 American troops soon expanded under President Clinton to include the capture of the Somali "warlord" Muhammad Farah Aidid. In October 1993 eighteen Army Rangers were killed in a firefight in Mogadishu, and scenes of some of the bodies being dragged through the streets appeared on American television. That caused a "CNN effect," and public sentiment turned against the operation, which was already suffering from amorphous "mission creep." Nevertheless, with a new president, William Jefferson

Clinton, and a secretary of defense, Les Aspin, whom the military did not respect, senior military officers were able to portray the October debacle as a failure of political leadership, not of military strategy or tactics. As a result, the Somalia operation weakened public confidence in the Clinton administration but did not lead to public skepticism of the capability and efficiency of the military.[26]

Further, the hesitation of the United States to intervene in Haiti in 1993 and 1994 was also interpreted by the public as a political rather than a military problem. The eventual decision to deploy American forces to restore Jean-Baptiste Aristide to the Haitian presidency and the peaceful resolution of the crisis further enhanced the image of the military as an effective tool of civilian policy, with all its failings due to civilian, rather than military, blunders.

At the same time, the deployment of U.S. forces to monitor and enforce the Dayton Agreement among the Bosnians, Serbs, and Croats was perceived as yet another successful use of force, with very little loss of life. In the Middle East, the United States continued to spar with Iraq and Saddam Hussein, and in the spring and fall of 1998 it appeared that U.S. air strikes against Iraqi targets were imminent. Although there was a great deal of public skepticism about the utility of bombing Iraq, the ability of the military to carry out its mission was never questioned. Iraq, Afghanistan, and Sudan were attacked with U.S. missiles, with dubious effect. Several neighborhoods of Baghdad were damaged, and a factory in Sudan that produced baby food, mistakenly identified as a chemical weapons plant, was obliterated. But the onus of blame fell on the White House, not the Pentagon, and certainly not the military in the field. Subsequent debates focused entirely on the political wisdom of an attack, not on the military capability. That was a quiet but forceful testimony to the depth of public satisfaction with the military.

In the spring of 1999, NATO air strikes in Kosovo once again demonstrated the capabilities of the U.S. military in succeeding on the battlefield. After a seventy-eight-day bombing campaign (led by U.S. forces) against military targets in Yugoslavia,

President Slobodan Milosevic agreed to withdraw his military forces from Kosovo and to allow NATO troops to occupy the region to ensure the return of ethnic Albanians. The Kosovo campaign reinforced the impression of a military able to mount campaigns swiftly, effectively, and with minimal casualties.

At the time of printing, U.S. troops are deployed in Afghanistan and in other locales around the world to hunt international terrorists. The swift overthrow of the Taliban government responsible for sheltering the terrorists and victories in hard-fought battles high in Afghanistani mountains are widely seen as successes for the military, especially the special forces, the CIA, and the Air Force. But Osama bin Laden and most of the Al Qaeda and Taliban leadership remain at large, a factor that casts some doubt on the effectiveness of the current operations. As the Bush administration continues to send troops to other trouble spots and terrorist-friendly locations, only time will tell whether the military can continue to perform up to the high standards of its most recent missions.

The story of the military since 1968 is a saga of an institution confronting its failures and accepting that dramatic change was imperative to its health and to the health of the society that it protects. After more than a decade of decline and tumbling morale, the armed forces began to regroup and then to restore the bonds of public confidence in the 1980s and 1990s. A series of highly successful operations demonstrated that the Vietnam War would be the exception, not the norm, and the Gulf War dispelled many, though not all, of the debilitating effects of the Vietnam syndrome. As we enter the third millennium, the U.S. armed forces remain highly popular. It seems clear that a direct relationship exists between that history and the current esteem in which the military is held and that an equally strong correlation exists between the performance of the military on the battlefield and public confidence in it.

4

Professionalism

A well-trained all-volunteer force that has arguably become more skilled with each passing year has carried out the military's successes over the past two decades. The noncommissioned officers are better trained, and many of the volunteers now see the military as a career rather than as an obligatory duty. The all-volunteer force has blossomed, and the 1970s problems with retention have receded. Once much criticized, the all-volunteer force has become the most visible symbol of the military's professionalism.

The end of the draft in 1973, highly controversial at the time, was an important step in military reform. At the very nadir of military morale and public confidence, a momentous change was introduced. While it would take almost a decade before the seeds sown by the all-volunteer force bore fruit, its creation ushered in a new era of military professionalism. From the most senior general and admiral of the fleet, to company-grade officers, and down through the ranks to noncommisioned officers and raw recruits, the military has come to be defined by high levels of skill, dedication, and discipline.

To some degree, public confidence in the military is a result of the professionalism exhibited on the battlefield. But while the battlefield is the most publicized and visible aspect, what the armed forces have done day to day is at least as momentous, both for the internal cohesion of the services and for public perceptions. Military professionalism has not simply been demonstrated in the Persian Gulf or Kosovo. It has also been evident in the way that the institution has responded to social problems.

The armed forces, like other organizations, face social challenges that interfere with the ability to achieve intended objectives. Yet the military seems to have met and answered those challenges and done so with far better results than the society as a whole. That has added to military effectiveness, but it also has enhanced the reputation of the military. The way that the various services have met those social challenges helps explain why trust in the military has risen so precipitately.

Like society at large, the military has had to deal with intractable issues such as race, gender integration, and the use of illegal drugs. Drug abuse threatens performance of troops on and off the battlefield, where soldiers have to be at their top physical and mental shape to complete their mission.

The end of conscription in the early 1970s required that the armed forces recruit individuals from all segments of American society, including a greater number of African Americans and women. Without those individuals, the military would not be able achieve its recruitment goals. Therefore, the military had to find effective ways to incorporate women and blacks into its ranks.

Civilian policymakers have been grappling with problems of race and gender integration as well as drug abuse for decades, but government agencies seem to have made less progress than the armed forces in addressing the problems. The military's response has displayed to the public the institution's professionalism and efficiency in confronting challenges in a manner that does not threaten the integrity or mission of the organization.

The Military and Drugs

In its handling of illegal drug use, the military's record of accomplishment far surpasses that of the civilian justice system or Twelve Step programs. That fact has not been lost on the general public. Thirty years ago, drug use threatened to undermine the ability of the military to carry out its missions. Today, that is no longer the case.

One of the more striking and disturbing developments during the later stages of the Vietnam War was the rampant use of drugs by American soldiers. For many, the image of GIs under the influence of drugs in the jungles was in itself sufficient reason to question the whole effort in Vietnam. In *Apocalypse Now*, soldiers take LSD during a Vietcong raid, and the entire scene becomes one undifferentiated mass of confused sights and sounds. That image did not originate with Francis Ford Coppola, the movie's director. It was taken directly from the military's own alarming reports.

In 1967 the Army registered no use of hallucinogenic drugs. But in 1971, according to the Army's own surveys, nearly 15 percent of enlistees had taken hallucinogenic drugs while on tour in Vietnam, nearly 23 percent had used heroin, 20 percent had used opium, and 60 percent had used marijuana. So severe was the problem that congressional committees investigated the effect of drug use on unit cohesiveness and military competency and in the process discovered that alcoholism was also pervasive.[1]

During the Vietnam War, so many soldiers were either addicted or habitual drug users that the military could not afford to discipline users too harshly, and it certainly could not afford a zero-tolerance policy. If everyone who used drugs had been punished according to the letter of law, units would have been decimated. The wink-and-nod approach reflected not cynicism but desperation.

Drug use in the military in the early and mid-1970s mirrored drug use in the larger society, particularly in the case of marijuana. During those years, drug use did not carry the same social stigma that it does in the 1990s, and civilian law enforcement tended to be lax in the case of marijuana and even of hallucinogens. Although soldiers in Vietnam used heroin and opium extensively, those drugs were stigmatized even in the general society in the 1970s, and the military focused on treatment programs designed to get soldiers to overcome addiction to those drugs. That meant a benign neglect of marijuana and alcohol abuse.

Given the multitude of challenges that confronted the military in the 1970s, drugs did not rank at the top of the list of priorities. Drug use was perceived as a symptom of low morale, and public

Figure 4-1 Trends in Illicit Drug Use in the Past Thirty Days for the Entire Department of Defense, 1980–1998

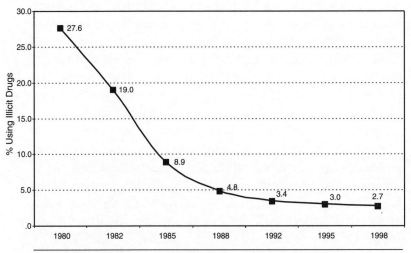

Source: Bray (1999).

attitudes in those years tended to be so permissive about drugs that military officials were concerned about cracking down too hard. With the onset of the all-volunteer force, the military could not afford to be seen as somehow disconnected from the larger society. It needed to draw volunteers, and a harsh drug policy might have sent a signal that military culture was far removed from American culture in general. At the same time, however, the military could not afford to tolerate drug use without jeopardizing mission effectiveness. Caught in that bind, the services began to experiment with ways of eliminating the problem.

After 1980, drug use began a steady decline in the military (see figure 4-1), almost in inverse proportion to the rise of defense budgets and improved military morale. President Ronald Reagan and First Lady Nancy Reagan were outspoken opponents of the drug culture, and their attitude of zero tolerance made it easier for military officials to adopt a similar approach. In 1982 the armed forces began mandatory drug testing. Soldiers were told that they could be tested randomly and at any time. If the tests showed positive for illegal substances, both officers and enlisted personnel faced harsh disciplinary action, including dishonorable discharge and prison time. As testing became more common, punishment became more Draconian. Soon it was standard practice to discharge anyone who tested positive.

According to former secretary of defense Casper Weinberger, the zero-tolerance policy worked in the 1980s because the response was swift and immediate. "The most effective deterrent of all," he wrote, "was the certain knowledge that all who were caught using drugs in any form would be immediately discharged. Morale was so high, and the desire to stay in the service was, and is, so great that the threat of automatic dismissal was the most effective control the services had."[2] Where the military brass had been wary of cracking down during the early years of the all-volunteer force, Weinberger recognized that the all-volunteer force actually allowed the military to take a strong stance. During the draft, drug use was an easy way for soldiers to rebel against an unpopular war and an unpopular military. But the all-volunteer force changed the nature of soldiers. Now, soldiers joined the military because they wanted the job, the career, and the skills. In the new world of the all-volunteer force, the risk of losing a desirable career surpassed the transitory lure of recreational drug use.

Of course, military policies toward drugs were not quite as smoothly implemented as Weinberger suggested. Early on, the tests were not always reliable, and errors could wreak havoc with a soldier's career. Tests were also not rigorously implemented. A Navy plane crashed on the aircraft carrier *Nimitz* in 1981, and its pilot was found to have eleven times the maximum limit for barbiturates in his blood. Yet even after that episode, testing itself was sometimes seen as a stigma, regardless of the results.

In time the Navy in particular developed a superb screening program that was a model of both efficiency and randomness. Personnel were screened on the basis of a sampling of Social Security numbers, and as the science became more refined, the minimum levels for drugs such as cocaine were dropped low enough to detect even minimal use. All the services also instituted rigorous testing to ensure that false negatives were caught and that false positives could be corrected before adversely affecting an innocent soldier.[3]

By the mid-1990s, drug use in the military had fallen dramatically from the levels of the 1970s, to the point where it was significantly less of a problem within the military than in the larger society. Alcohol abuse programs also reduced the incidents of alcohol-related problems. Although the severity of punishment for testing positive clearly was a major deterrent, the military also set up extensive counseling facilities and treatment programs for soldiers who came forth voluntarily to admit to an addiction. The stricture was harshest against those caught by random testing, but like companies in the general workforce, the military made allowances for human failing and to some degree accommodated those who on their own took steps to end a drug addiction.[4]

Indeed, from 1980 through 1998, the health habits of military personnel improved markedly, according to surveys conducted by the Research Triangle Institute. Besides the decline in illicit drugs shown in figure 4-1, heavy alcohol use declined from 20.8 percent in 1980 to 15.4 percent in 1998, while cigarette smoking decreased from 51.0 percent of personnel in 1980 to 29.9 percent in 1998.[5]

Little direct evidence exists that military efforts to eliminate illegal drug use have led to increased public confidence. But in the 1980s and to a lesser but still significant degree in the 1990s and into the first decade of the new millennium, drug use remains a prevalent concern in the larger society. Parents, school boards, and politicians are forever discussing how to cut down on illegal drugs, and Presidents Clinton and Bush have been unequivocal about their commitment to combat the spread of illegal drugs. The fact that the military has successfully contained drug use has been widely publicized. But the methods the military uses are not easily applicable in civilian life. Constitutional protections make it difficult to institute random testing outside of college athletics, and the public is deeply divided on the question of punishment and job loss versus treatment. Still, the public views the military as one institution that has solved a problem that in every other area of American society is seen as unsolvable.

Racial Integration

In addition to reducing the use of illegal drugs, the military has made significant progress in achieving racial integration. While currently the larger society continues to grapple with the most effective way of addressing America's racial problems, the military has been quietly confronting and surmounting the issue.

Although President Harry S Truman issued an executive order in 1948 desegregating the armed services, racial problems were one of the most destabilizing aspects of the military's crisis in the late 1960s and early 1970s. On military bases, housing discrimination skirmishes between white and black enlisted men and a wide variety of discriminatory practices were common. In 1969 at Camp Lejeune in North Carolina, riots between white and black Marines resulted in the death of a white corporal. Although a congressional investigatory committee concluded that the violence was primarily a reflection of racial tensions within the United States at the time and not of any particular Marine Corps policies, the Marine commandant publicly acknowledged that "a serious racial problem" existed in the military. In response, the Marine Corps instituted classes designed to enhance awareness of racial problems, and the Army did so as well.[6]

At the end of 1970, Defense Secretary Melvin Laird made public a report on poor race relations that found that the primary cause was "the failure in too many instances of command leadership to exercise its authority and responsibility." The report also documented numerous instances of discrimination in military justice, promotions, work assignments, and housing.

Faced with intractable racial divisions in the late 1960s, military leaders concluded that so long as those divisions persisted and even worsened, the military's effectiveness would be seriously compromised. Service chiefs, therefore, saw racial problems not as a social issue per se but rather as a crisis of the military's ability to get the job done—a crisis that came to a head during the Vietnam War. But the recognition that racial integration was essential did not immediately translate into genuine racial integration. As with most challenges, things got worse before they got better.

Race and the All-Volunteer Force. Race was a major factor in the deterioration of unit cohesion in Vietnam. Combined with rampant drug use, flagrant disregard and disrespect for officers by enlisted men, and a general malaise triggered by the sense that the American public did not support the war, the quality of the military as a fighting force declined. It was then that the services and civilian officials began to look seriously at abolishing the draft. One of the initial objections to the all-volunteer force was that the racial balance in the enlisted ranks would tip. That was a polite way of expressing fear that the military would become too black. Some whites, viewing blacks through the lens of racial prejudice, worried that the quality of the armed forces would decline as the proportion of blacks rose. Black leaders, for their part, were troubled because they feared that the all-volunteer force was simply a way to get young black men—rather than affluent, white Americans—to fight and die. The all-volunteer force was not phased in until the war in Vietnam was all but phased out. Initially, the proportion of black enlistees did not rise precipitately, but by 1976, it was clear that the composition of the enlisted troops was changing significantly. Far fewer college graduates enlisted; many enlistees came from the lower end of the socioeconomic scale; and a rising proportion of soldiers were, in fact, African American. By 1979, more than a third of enlisted volunteers in the Army were African American, nearly triple the percentage of blacks in the population as a whole and nearly triple the percentage in the Army in 1969. The percentages were significantly lower in the Navy and the Air Force, apparently because those branches did not recruit minorities as heavily.[7]

By the early 1980s, the worst racial tensions lay in the past, but the composition of the military worried some—and not just because of racial prejudice. In 1983 Senator Ernest Hollings of South Carolina expressed his concern that the all-volunteer force had created a military that was not representative of American society. Speaking to a group of Dartmouth College students, Hollings declared, "I want to draft everyone in this room for the good of the country. . . . Conscience tells us that we need a cross-section of America in our armed forces. Defense is everybody's business." Representative Paul Simon of Illinois echoed that sentiment. He said that the United States was relying too heavily on the poor to fight its battles and die for the country.[8]

Insofar as the military enlisted ranks drew heavily from lower income groups, the developments of the 1970s and 1980s were nothing new. The armed forces in the United States have always depended disproportionately on those less well-off financially. The shift in racial composition was different, however, and although Hollings and Simon may have expressed their discomfort with the racial changes in economic terms, it was not the first time that racial fears had been discussed indirectly.

Compounding those concerns, the new enlistees scored less well on performance tests and entered with less formal education than had been the case in decades past. Into the early 1980s, only 7 percent of military volunteers had some college experience, compared with 15 percent in the 1960s. African American enlistees scored lower than their white counterparts on the Armed Forces Qualification Test, and fewer of them had completed high school. Given that high school graduates of any race are more likely to complete their three-year term of service, African Americans in those years also showed higher levels of attrition than other groups of enlistees.[9]

Lower scores on performance tests led to a disproportionate number of African Americans serving in nontechnical jobs, such as clerks and supply handlers. The service branches made an effort to reduce the proportion of blacks serving in combat units, largely from sensitivity to the charges that blacks were being asked to perform tasks that might result in loss of life more frequently than whites or other ethnic groups. At the same time, while a significant percentage of blacks in the 1970s and early 1980s did serve in combat units, their combat service did not lead to rapid increases in the number of black officers. African American servicemen still tended to be grouped in the lower ranks, and, again, part of the reason for that was the performance of blacks on the standardized tests used to evaluate personnel for promotion.

The difficulty blacks have had advancing to company-grade officers mirrors the problems blacks have had gaining admittance to selective colleges and graduate schools in the greater society. As a group, African Americans do not perform as well on standardized tests, and for some of those tests, such as the Scholastic Aptitude Test, that has led to widespread questioning of the fairness of the exams. The same questions have been raised about the fairness of military performance exams, and as it became apparent in the early 1980s that lower scores were keeping blacks from rising through the ranks in proportion to their numbers, the services began to consider changing the litmus test for evaluating performance.

The Army itself, in internal studies, questioned whether the tests might be racially biased. In a 1981 report, an Army commission studying the tests reported that certain vocabulary questions "disproportionately reflected a cultural background typical of the majority male population of white test-takers."[10] As a result of its findings, the Army intensified its efforts to equalize racial imbalances in promotion and job distribution. Without saying so directly, the Army committed itself to a wide-ranging affirmative action program. Notably, however, black officers showed the greatest *improvement* in SAT scores from 1976 to 1990. The Army's successes were likely due to heavy recruiting into the officer corps and through the expanded use of the U.S. Military Academy Preparatory School, based at Fort Monmouth, New Jersey.[11]

The subject of affirmative action within the military is touchy. In light of the widespread controversies surrounding affirmative action in the larger society, military officials are reluctant to address the advancement of blacks in the armed services in terms of affirmative action.[12] *Affirmative action* as a term carries the stigma that merit is sacrificed in the interest of racial balance. The armed services emphatically reject the notion that there has been any lessening of standards to promote more African American officers and noncommissioned officers. During the late 1970s and early 1980s, a large number of military leaders struggled to arrive at a method for promoting African Americans in particular without lowering standards in general. Their attitude toward sacrificing standards might be summed up as "If we lower the bar, people die." The fact that military missions involve life and death in the most immediate and literal sense meant that unlike college admissions or promotions within government bureaucracies, lowering standards in the military truly could place lives in jeopardy.

At the same time, many company-grade officers realized that even if the spirit of the standards was not biased, the application of them often was. Far too many blacks in the military testified to the frequent and repeated violations of equal opportunity regulations, and the subtle but pervasive climate of distrust of blacks and favoritism of whites. While the armed forces by the early 1980s could no longer be accused of institutional racism, the evidence of individual racism and bias was far too extensive for the military commanders to ignore. Black enlistees were often punished or held back for behavior or violations that were overlooked in white soldiers, and they were excluded from the informal network for promotions that disproportionately benefited white soldiers.[13]

In the 1980s, under the leadership of General Maxwell Thurman, military recruitment policies were reviewed, and changes were implemented. As General John Galvin remarked, "Max Thurman's initiatives made a vast difference in race relations in these years."[14] Until the early 1980s, recruitment inducements were primarily economic. The military tried to use monetary lures to get young Americans to enlist. Under Thurman's direction, however, the military started to focus more on educational benefits, especially postservice benefits such as money for college. Asked about how important those benefits were in their decision to enlist, 51 percent of blacks and 32 percent of whites said "important" or "very important."

By moving away from the emphasis on the military as a good way to earn a living, Thurman was able to attract a different type of recruit. That does not mean that African American recruits before 1980 were necessarily less motivated, but the closer connection between education and military service seems to have raised the level of dedication among all soldiers.[15] And as recruitment policies and patterns evolved, so did racial attitudes within the military.

Between 1970 and 1990, the number of black officers and senior noncommissioned officers in the Army rose dramatically, from 14 percent in 1970 to 26 percent in 1980 to 31 percent in 1990. For commissioned officers, the change was from 3 percent in 1970 to 7 percent in 1980 to 11 percent in 1990.

With the rise of the all-volunteer military, the Army began a concerted effort to draw more minorities into its officer corps through its own preparatory academy. The U.S. Military Academy Preparatory School is a one-year school for students who have graduated from high school but who are not likely to be admitted directly to West Point. Given that West Point remains the most significant source of company-grade officers, black officers were at a relative disadvantage for highly competitive promotions so long as relatively few of them were admitted to West Point. The U.S. Military Academy Preparatory School, founded in 1916, has long been a preparatory school for West Point, but in recent years almost a quarter of its annual class of 200 has been African American. In any given year, West Point accepts about two-thirds of the graduates from that preparatory academy. The U.S. Military Academy Preparatory School has helped not only black high school graduates who otherwise would not have qualified for West Point but also black enlisted men who could not earn high enough scores on admissions tests such as the SAT to gain admission to West Point. After a year at the U.S. Military Academy Preparatory School, black cadets performed nearly as well on standardized tests as their white peers.[16]

Figure 4-2 High School Seniors Who Say That They "Want to Serve in the Armed Forces," by Race, 1976–2000

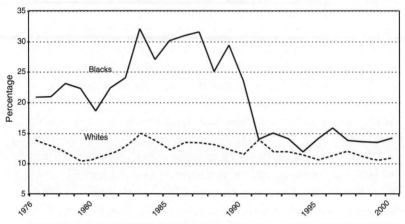

Source: Johnston, Bachman, and O'Malley (1998).

In addition to the U.S. Military Academy Preparatory School, the Army began to recruit more heavily from Reserve Officers' Training Corps programs at historically black colleges. The result was that by the 1990s, one in nine Army officers was black, and 24 of 328 generals were black. The appointment of Colin Powell as the first African American chairman of the Joint Chiefs of Staff, as well as the appointment of Togo West as secretary of the Army in 1993, signified that African Americans could rise to the highest echelons of both the civilian and military leadership.

The Powell Factor. The improvements were undeniable, but as the larger society shifted, the military successes did not translate into unequivocal popularity. The white community embraced General Powell, but many blacks viewed him skeptically, especially young black males. It is a puzzle just why Powell did not resonate with young blacks, but his time as chairman of the Joint Chiefs, 1989 through 1993, coincides with a precipitate drop in the willingness of black high school seniors to consider joining the armed forces. (See figure 4-2.)

First noted by David Segal and Jerald Bachman, the drop in willingness to serve came in 1991, the last year in Segal and Bachman's analysis. They speculated that the drop "may have been influenced by opposition to the Gulf War, which was higher in black than in white communities, and by a renewal in black communities of the debate that emerged in the early years of the all-volunteer force about whether the overrepresentation of African Americans in the Army reflected an employment opportunity or an unfair burden."[17]

The dip in willingness to serve among black high school students persisted throughout the 1990s. During the 1980s, blacks were twice as likely as whites to say, "I want to serve in the armed forces." During the 1990s, blacks and whites have had virtually the same propensities. It may be that the economic boom of the 1990s made the military a less attractive career choice for African Americans. Although the economic gains of the "New Economy" were not nearly as evident in African American communities, it is still true that with economic prosperity the military has had a hard time competing. While it offered unparalleled benefits, it also did not hold the prospect of a remunerative career, and in the heart of the 1990s, the allure of quick wealth undermined the military's ability to recruit.

Powell's popularity and his high public profile focused public attention on the military and race. Although some of his critics accused him of dodging his racial identity to advance, throughout his career his attitude toward race and the military was clear. He identified himself as an American, an officer, and an African American—in that order. Speaking at Howard University in May 1993, he recalled the efforts of the buffalo soldiers and the Tuskegee airmen. "I will never forget my debt to them," he said. "I didn't just show up. I climbed on the backs of those who never had the kind of opportunity I had. I will never forget. You must never forget."[18] In his autobiography, *My American Journey,* Powell was outspoken about the struggle of racial minorities in the military to overcome a legacy of institutional and individual prejudice. That autobiography sold millions of copies, and its central themes were disseminated to millions more through Powell's speeches and his many appearances on television and radio after his retirement and leading up to the presidential election in 1996. Although he declined to run for president in 1996, his appointment as secretary of state in the Bush administration in 2001 only solidified his story as an unqualified success for the military's policy of identifying qualified racial minorities and promoting them.

In many ways, Powell is the apogee of race relations in the all-volunteer military. His careful defense of affirmative action contrasted starkly with the Republican platform of 1996, and yet his popularity far transcended that of the GOP nominee, Robert J. Dole. Evidence suggests that people supported Powell because he was an example of the successes of affirmative action. While Powell expressed discomfort with quotas and racial preferences that glossed over deficient skills, he quietly championed a vision of affirmative action that emphasizes that each person is responsible for clearing the same bar, even if certain groups are given more training and preparation to help them do so.[19]

In talking about his career, Powell struck a balance that many Americans felt was absent in discussions of race in the larger society. He was able simultaneously to recognize the obstacles that racism placed in the way of black advancement and to demand of himself and everyone else that they meet the demands placed on them, whether in the form of standardized tests and combat skills or in civilian life.

Understanding Colin Powell's appeal is central to understanding the popularity of the military in the 1990s as it has evolved into what some have called America's social laboratory. Although his performance as a general during the Gulf War and his questionable assertion of authority relative to the White House continue to be debated, for the public at large those are nonissues. People either do not know or do not particularly care about whether and how Colin Powell overstepped his proper role as chairman of the Joint Chiefs of Staff by writing for policy journals and newspapers. And they were sufficiently disenchanted with Clinton in 1993 that they sided with Powell rather than the

Clinton administration on those issues where Powell differed from his civilian commanders. What people did know, and what they expressed in 1996, was that Powell seemed to have squared the circle of race, standards, and affirmative action. And he was so clearly and proudly a product of military culture that people could not help but hold a great deal of confidence in an organization that produced a man like Colin Powell.

Powell also reflected the changes that occurred in the way African American soldiers viewed both the military and the larger society. According to surveys conducted in the early 1990s, black soldiers are twice as likely as black civilians to be satisfied with their jobs. In fact, as Charles Moskos and John Sibley Butler pointed out, black soldiers are actually more satisfied with their jobs than white civilians are with theirs. Addressing why this is so, Moskos and Butler concluded that military blacks trust that they will be rewarded for their work (if it is done well), that there is less likelihood in the military than in civilian life that they will be consigned to less prestigious work, and that by its very nature, military work inculcates high levels of self-esteem.[20]

Blacks in the military also have a more optimistic picture of race relations in general than blacks in the civilian world. Black soldiers report that their view of other races improved after they entered the military, and white soldiers confirm that impression and respond that they too developed a better impression of non-whites after enlisting. In fact, black soldiers have significantly shaped the culture of enlisted men, in seemingly innocuous ways such as the music enlisted men listen to and the way that they speak. Those subtle cultural changes reflect the extent to which integration is a fact in today's military.

Indeed, although the willingness of young blacks to join the military is now the same as young whites' willingness, young blacks and Hispanics are overrepresented in recruit demographics. While a general recruitment problem emerged again in the late 1990s, including a declining willingness of young blacks to enlist, among the cohort that did enlist, minorities and blacks are disproportionately represented. In fiscal year 1999 the percentages of new recruits who were black were 24 percent in the Army, 20 percent in the Navy, 13 percent in the Marines, and 17 percent in the Air Force. In each instance those percentages are larger than the black percentage in the population as a whole. Likewise, Hispanics made up 12 percent, 15 percent, 13 percent, and 7 percent of the 1999 recruiting classes for the same services.[21] Only the Air Force, which is notable for *not* actively recruiting minorities, lags behind.

True, the percentage of black officers continues to fall short relative to the percentage of African Americans as a whole in the services. But a majority of people in the military seem to feel that as the programs instituted in the late 1970s and 1980s continue to bear fruit, more junior African American officers will get promoted at all levels from senior noncommissioned officers through company-grade officers.

So has the military solved the problem of race? No. But even when problems remain, the public perception is that the armed forces do a better job addressing those problems than any other part of society. In the 1990s, some civilian commentators interpreted the sexual scandals involving allegations of rape of enlisted women by black sergeants at the Aberdeen Proving Ground as evidence of continued racial bias in the military. In the wake of the bombing of the federal building in Oklahoma City in 1995, a number of small groups of white separatist soldiers were detected on various military bases. Some saw those incidents as an indication that racism and race hatred still prevail in the military. Yet few African American soldiers and few Americans in the larger society seem to have interpreted matters in that way. Judging from numerous surveys, the first scandals were viewed by the public as part of a broader tension over women in the military. As for the presence of small numbers of white separatists within the military, that was taken to indicate tension within the United States as a whole, not within the military in particular.

The sexual scandals of the 1990s military, however, point to another area where the services have faced severe challenges and where they have, at least in the mind of many Americans, done an admirable job of coming to terms with the changes wrought by the sexual revolution of the 1960s. In short, while much work remains to be done, a significant percentage of the American public believes that the military has not just done a good job integrating the races; it has also gained respect for how it has tried to integrate women into the armed forces.

Women in the Military

In some sense, the operative word here is *tried*. Gender integration remains a heated and unresolved issue in the military. As Charles Moskos wrote in the *Washington Post,* people frequently ask why the Army, which has done so well with racial integration, still struggles so intensely with gender integration. But Moskos and many others feel that the comparison is inappropriate. While no significant physiological differences exist between the races, they do between the sexes. In addition, while most Americans agree that racial equality is both necessary and desirable, both men and women are divided on the issue of gender equality. Although Moskos firmly has advocated gender integration in the armed services, he believes that the reason such integration has been harder to achieve is that the issues are more complex than they are with race.[22] While many would disagree with Moskos's tone, even a cursory glance at the legacy of women in the military over the past three decades demonstrates just how complex the issues are.

When the draft ended at the close of the Vietnam War, there were only 45,000 women in the military, or about 2 percent of the total. During the war itself, women served as nurses and emergency relief personnel, roles that they had traditionally occupied in the previous two conflicts.

One of the effects of the all-volunteer force was to create a manpower vacuum; recruiters scrambled to maintain force levels as the supply of recruits shrank overnight. At about the same time, Congress passed the Equal Rights Amendment in 1972,[23] and members of the House Armed Services Committee criticized the military's resistance to having more women serve. As a result of both that amendment and the all-volunteer force, the services began to recruit women actively. The desperate need to meet recruitment quotas trumped the traditional notion of the military as a male bastion. Although women were rigidly excluded from combat functions, they were easily assigned to noncombat tasks. Between 1972 and 1976, the number of women in uniform grew to 109,000, which amounted to 5 percent of the total.[24]

As more women entered the ranks, however, the services found it increasingly untenable to restrict their activities to a few select jobs. There were too many women and too few of the jobs defined as "noncombat," and with the theme of women's liberation echoing throughout the country, the military felt some public relations pressure to accommodate women's ambitions to be more than cooks, cleaners, and secretaries. In 1976 the General Accounting Office recommended that each branch of the armed forces develop physical standards for its jobs, including minimum strength and stamina requirements. The same report suggested that the services think of ways to open more jobs to women than had been available in the past.[25]

But that did not mute the criticism. If anything, the debate intensified. The 1970s in general were a time of immense flux in relations between the sexes and in women's identities. Until the mid-1960s, social debate over the proper role of women in the armed forces had been muted and at times almost nonexistent. Although World War II saw large numbers of women in the services, once there they performed traditional support roles, and when the war ended, they left the military and returned to civilian life. But after the Vietnam War, civilian life for women was far more fluid and undefined than it had been after World War II, and some women saw the restrictions on what jobs women could perform in the military as yet another indication of their second-class status in society.

Women as well as men, however, were divided about just how "equal" men and women could be in the military. The debate then as now comes down to biology: are women capable, physically, of fighting as effectively as men? No one questions that men tend, on average, to be stronger than women, but what limits that puts on women's ability to fight and kill continues to be hotly argued. In addition, women and men are divided about whether they even support the notion of women fighting and killing. Images of what it means to be a woman in American society still do not include women with guns, fatigues, and knives (the occasional Hollywood fantasy notwithstanding), or women in the cockpits of Air Force fighters, or women in bunks above men in submarines for six months at a time.

In 1971 less than a quarter of those polled by Roper agreed with the statement that "women should have equal treatment regarding the draft." A year later, nearly two-thirds said that they were opposed or very opposed to the idea of women's military service. And in 1973 three-quarters of respondents in the Detroit area agreed, "If anyone should bear arms, it should be men rather than women."[26] During the 1970s, political feminists were split in their attitudes toward women in the military. Some viewed the presence of women as a positive development and as a strong signal that women should not be barred from any activity simply because of their gender. Others, however, saw the development as a step back. Significant numbers of feminists in the 1970s were also pacifists who had adamantly opposed the Vietnam War, and they did not see the presence of women in the military as any more preferable to men in the military. Others stressed that while equality of opportunity was vital, women and men are different, and one thing that makes women who they are is that they do not have a proclivity to kill in the way men do. Those feminists believed that women who fought in the military were regressing, not progressing. Still others suggested that women in the military, while they would inevitably "mirror" some traditionally male values by embracing a warrior code, could also subtly transform that code. Just as black soldiers influenced the culture of white soldiers, so too women would "feminize" the army in positive ways.[27] This last perspective was deeply troubling to many men in the military.

As more women were recruited, Congress also required the services to admit women to the service academies. At first, the services resisted. They asserted that the academies trained the future company-grade officers, and company-grade officers were usually combat officers. Women were not eligible for combat duty, and so, argued the service chiefs, they ought not to be trained for careers that they could not have. Congress disagreed, and without changing the ban on women in combat, passed legislation in 1975 admitting women to the academies. With military morale at its nadir in those years, many commanders interpreted the influx of women as a sign that the old military order, with its traditional values of protecting women rather than fighting alongside them, was dying, and they resisted. Many male soldiers expressed resentment at the changes and attempted to curtail any expansion of women's roles beyond support staff.

In particular, the services refused to consider the possibility that women might be allowed into combat. Combat exclusion laws were first passed in 1948, and since then women in the Navy, Air Force, and Marines have been banned from full-time service on aircraft or ships whose primary mission is combat. The Army has fewer statutory limitations, but it too has kept women out of units that it defines as combat-oriented. In 1977 the secretary of the Army issued guidelines barring women from "close combat" units that had a high probability of direct physical engagement with an enemy. Those restrictions have never meant that women in the military do not get exposed to danger. Nurses, medical teams, and supply units have all suffered casualties during war, and women in the military died and were wounded in World War II, Korea, and Vietnam.[28] Those restrictions did prevent women from attaining positions of leadership within the armed forces.

The resistance of the services to further integration of women took several forms. Attitudes toward women remained highly traditional, and in the face of regulations designed to further equal opportunity, officers often passively ignored them. In doing so they could easily take the cue from the senior commanders and civilian officials at the time. In the mid-1970s a former superintendent of the Air Force Academy expressed a widely shared view. He said, "For this nation to open combat roles to our women, short of dire emergency . . . offends the dignity of womanhood and ignores the harsh realities of war." Others complained that integrating women would mean lowering standards and thereby compromising the effectiveness of the entire military. Six months into his term as Carter's secretary of defense, Harold Brown stated, "I believe there are sufficient physical differences between men and women, on the average, that make it wise, as regulations provide, that women not be put into combat roles." General William Westmoreland, senior commander in Vietnam from 1964 through 1968 and never a master of subtlety, said after he retired, "Maybe you could find one woman in 10,000 who could lead in combat, but she would be a freak, and we're not running the military academy for freaks."[29]

From the late 1970s through the early 1980s, attitudes about women in the military in general and in combat in particular were contradictory. Directed by the Carter administration to increase the percentage of women in the services to 15 percent by 1986, military officials took the election of Ronald Reagan as a sign that they might be able to freeze the further integration of women and perhaps even turn back some of the developments of the 1970s. Both the Army and the Air Force informed Congress in 1981 that they were cutting back on the quotas assigned by Carter. While some senior members of the Reagan administration were quite supportive of those actions, their cultural sympathy could not be squared with the problem of maintaining and increasing the desired force levels with an all-volunteer military.

President Reagan intended to expand the size of the armed forces, but he was adamantly opposed to restoring the draft for reasons of political expediency as much as anything else. As Lawrence Korb pointed out, if the military services had been allowed to freeze the number of women in the military at 171,000 in 1980, "it would have been almost impossible for the president to increase the size of the active duty force in an era of declining supply without compromising quality or returning to conscription."[30] One response to that reality was to develop a sophisticated advertising and marketing campaign, which we discuss later. Another was that, once again, the need for able bodies overruled the objections to recruiting more women.

Of course, not all soldiers objected. Many, in fact, embraced the notion of more women in the military, and some were more than willing to see women in combat. That reflected the position held by the population as a whole. In the 1982 General Social Survey, 93 percent of respondents approved of women serving as combat nurses. That number was predictable, given the roles women had frequently performed in the military in the past. The other numbers were more surprising, given the staunch resistance to change by the military brass. More than three-quarters of those surveyed supported the presence of women in what were called "nontraditional noncombat roles," such as mechanics and air transport personnel. Nearly 60 percent supported the idea of women base commanders. On women in combat roles, 62 percent were comfortable with women as fighter pilots, 59 percent supported women as missile gunners, 57 percent accepted the notion of women stationed on combat ships, and 35 percent felt that women could serve as ground combat troops. There were some interesting variances in those results, however. Black men were less likely to support women in nontraditional roles than were white men, and black women were also more traditional in their attitudes than were white women.[31]

Not for the last time, the attitudes of the military brass did not mirror attitudes prevalent in the society at large. The gap between civilian and military values was not widely discussed during the 1970s and 1980s, but as we later examine, it has become a troubling issue. In terms of gender integration, Congress slowly overcame those in the military trying to resist the changes, by the shifting attitudes of enlisted personnel and by necessity. More jobs were opened up to women, although the most dramatic change, that of allowing women to train as fighter pilots and stationing them on aircraft carriers, would not come until the mid-1990s. Throughout the 1980s the services offered a variety of objections to women in combat or more physically demanding noncombat roles. Some suggested that women were not psychologically able to carry out certain tasks, but most of the arguments centered on biology. First, there was the question whether women are physically able to perform certain roles. From uniforms to the configuration of hand-held missile launchers and aircraft cockpits, military equipment had been designed with the average man in mind. Any men whose measurements fell in the top or bottom 5 percent of all men were barred from certain tasks. Yet about 50 percent of all women in the Army, for instance, weigh less than a man in the fifth percentile and 60 percent are shorter.[32] Women also have less upper body strength than most men.

Because of physical discrepancies between the sexes, women were ineligible for most tasks associated with combat. As a case in point, the Army has a rigorous system for matching soldiers with tasks that they can physically perform. Through the 1980s, that system, known as "Military Occupational Specialty Physical Demands Analysis," was in theory gender-neutral, but the bar was sufficiently high that the majority of women could not clear it, while proportionately far more men could. The issue was not whether performance standards should be relaxed so as to allow women to qualify for such jobs, but rather whether the standards themselves precluded even a highly skilled woman from ever qualifying.[33]

Perhaps the most sensitive and fraught issue of women in the military is pregnant soldiers. At first, the military could not imagine how it could accommodate pregnant women on active duty. Until the 1970s, women who got pregnant were discharged or suspended from duty. In 1970 her commander discharged Anna Flores, a twenty-three-year-old unmarried seaman stationed at a naval air base in Florida, after she miscarried. The commander explained that to allow her to remain would have been tantamount to condoning pregnancy out of wedlock. Flores asked the U.S. District Court for an injunction. She claimed that the Navy was discriminating against women by discharging her and not her equally unwed paramour. The Navy relented in Flores's case, and other suits soon followed. In the early 1970s Captain Susan Struck, a pregnant nurse at an Air

Force base, refused to leave the service. Although the Air Force command was determined to fight Struck all the way to the Supreme Court, the solicitor general advised them that they would not win and that they ought to accommodate the captain. Finally, in 1974 the Department of Defense instructed the service that terminating a woman's active duty status or forcing her to resign as a result of pregnancy was no longer a viable option. Thereafter, the military would have to find ways to accommodate pregnant soldiers.[34]

Having made the concession that pregnant women could function in the military, the services next had to consider just how extensively women could be integrated. Should there be mixed-gender training? Mixed-gender units? Women in all combat positions? Young men and women in integrated basic training? Each of those questions was studied intensively, and consensus proved elusive. Military women were almost as divided as military men. One added issue was that if women were to be allowed to serve in combat, did that also mean that civilian women would be required to register for the draft and therefore be subject to conscription in wartime? Many civilian women did not like the notion of registering for selective service, and many did not support the notion of women in combat. Yet within the military that ban kept women from advancing through the ranks, except as company-grade officers in noncombat assignments such as nursing, support, quartermaster, and the like.

Throughout the 1980s, as more women joined the services, those issues remained unresolved, and they continued to be unresolved in the 1990s. By 1998, almost imperceptibly, women had come to serve in almost every job imaginable, with only a few, albeit significant, restrictions on ground combat, submarines, and assorted other high-intensity combat jobs. Most women, both in the military and in the general population, do not support the mandatory assignment of women to combat roles, but the majority is in favor of allowing women to volunteer for combat. Many military women believe that standards can be different and should remain different for men and women and that such differences rarely have a negative impact on fighting effectiveness.[35]

The Gulf War: A Turning Point. The 1991 Gulf War was in many ways a turning point for public and military attitudes toward women in combat. Nearly 40,000 women were sent to the Gulf, thirteen women were killed, and there were even female prisoners of war. Throughout the conflict, the public by large margins supported the presence of women in the Gulf. After the war, in 1992, a president's commission voted against lifting the combat exclusion and effectively continued to keep women out of combat situations. Defense secretary Les Aspin, however, forced through a directive that put women on aircraft carriers and opened many combat-support jobs to women, such as certain types of engineering, military intelligence, and military police tasks. By 1993, 97 percent of Air Force military occupational specialties were open to women, 61 percent in the Army, 60 percent in the Navy, and 34 percent in the Marine Corps. Interestingly, women in all the services were eligible to learn skills for positions for which they were not (yet) technically eligible because of training schedules.[36]

As part of the argument in favor of opening up hitherto restricted positions, advocates of lifting the combat exclusions looked to the example of other countries, such as Israel and Canada, which did not have the same barriers. In 1987 Canadian forces opened all combat positions to women, except for submarines. Yet in Canada women also had to pass the same physical requirements as the men, a requirement that severely restricted the number of women eligible for combat. In the United States a frequent objection to women in ground combat has been that unit effectiveness would suffer. It was said that male soldiers would spend more time worrying about the safety of the women than in carrying out the mission and that the integrity of the unit might be compromised. Yet in those few countries where there have been mixed units, the evidence sometimes points in the opposite direction. Women compete harder to earn the respect of the men, while the men work harder so as not to be overshadowed by the women. Male soldiers have shown a marked tendency toward chivalry in their dealings with female soldiers; they help women in ways that they would not help other men. At the same time, male soldiers have also shown a marked tendency to harass female soldiers in ways that they would not harass other men.[37]

The presence of men and women in mixed units sparked concerns that sexual harassment would become endemic. As women became more integrated into the military, new attention was focused on relations between the sexes. Since the late 1970s, the military services had experimented with different ways to regulate sexual relations between the sexes. In the 1980s units began to hold seminars similar to the seminars for easing integration between the races.

In the early 1990s what had been primarily an internal military problem about harassment became a national issue with the Tailhook scandal, where an admiral's aide and former pilot were sexually assaulted during a convention for naval aviators in Las Vegas. Coming on the heels of the Clarence Thomas–Anita Hill imbroglio, the Tailhook affair received intense press and public scrutiny and led to congressional investigations about the status of women and gender relations in the military. Many observers believed that at its core, the Tailhook affair was the response of a Navy culture that had been willing to tolerate more women only so long as those women were kept out of combat roles. As women began to train as pilots and inch closer to full participation, there was a backlash.[38]

Although it is almost impossible to prove that the movement of women into combat or near combat roles created a backlash in the form of increased sexual harassment, the correlation is undeniable. After the Tailhook affair, political leaders instructed the military to integrate basic training, and following Aspin's decree in 1993, many of the walls keeping women from combat positions came tumbling down. While there are still remarkably few female admirals or generals, women have been stationed on aircraft carriers and are now serving as pilots in almost all types of aircraft, notably in the Navy and the Air Force.

The integration of basic training then led to a further series of sexual harassment scandals, as well as charges of widespread rape by training sergeants of recruits at an army base at the Aberdeen

Proving Ground and then allegations against the top enlisted man in the Army, Sergeant-Major Gene McKinney. While McKinney was found innocent of the most serious charges against him, several sergeants at Aberdeen were convicted of rape. Questions of fraternization, adultery, and the military code of ethics as applied to relations between soldiers remain charged topics, ones that engage not only the passions of the military but of the larger society.

For example, in 1997, Air Force Lieutenant Kelly Flinn became a lightning rod for discussions of adultery, ethics, and Air Force regulations. Flinn was dismissed for refusing to break off an affair with a married man and then lying about it to investigators. The Flinn episode, which flared into public consciousness and became the topic of the week on daytime talk shows and evening news magazines, was followed by other imbroglios. The nominee for chairman of the Joint Chiefs of Staff, General Joseph Ralston, withdrew his name from consideration because of an adulterous affair he had carried on ten years earlier. Three army officers at Fort Bliss, Texas, were sentenced to prison for sexual misconduct, and a female West Point cadet was found guilty of making false rape charges against a male cadet. All those cases became fodder for the twenty-four-hour news cycle.

Through all the incidents, public attitudes about the military have remained highly favorable. Americans did express pessimism that the military would ever root out sexual harassment, yet that did not dissuade most parents from allowing their daughters to enlist. Sixty-five percent of those asked in a February 1997 Associated Press poll said that the recent allegations of sexual misconduct did not constitute a sufficient reason to tell a daughter or the daughter of a friend not to join the military.[39] Indeed, among high school seniors, the willingness of women to join the military actually increased from 1994 to 1997.

It seems that many Americans feel that men and women sometimes do questionable things, and the fact that they do such things is a function of gender relations, not of military culture. Far from leading to public calls to halt the integration of women, those incidents were taken by the public as signals that the military is too puritanical and too rigid. Almost half the men and women surveyed in a June 1997 *Newsweek* poll responded that they felt that the military had gone too far in treating extramarital affairs as punishable offenses. And significant majorities felt that the punishment of Kelly Flinn was excessive. Surprisingly, 60 percent of women felt that the military should not treat it as a crime if a higher-ranking man has sexual relations with a lower-ranking woman.[40] Far from viewing the issue of sexual harassment and adultery as reasons to slow or reverse the integration of women in the military, most people believed that the scandals were simply bumps in the road, which, while unfortunate, should in no way be taken as a sign that the military is headed in the wrong direction.

The transformation of the role of women in American society in the late 1960s reshaped the military in the 1970s. At the same time, the changing technology of war made the biological differences between men and women less relevant. Few men or women contest that in terms of pure physical strength, men have an advantage over women. As long as warfare consisted primarily of brute contests of strength between opposing armies, the absolute injunction against women in combat was logical. Yet war today is waged for the most part by technologically advanced machines operated by soldiers. Even infantry units rarely engage each other in hand-to-hand combat. As a result of those technological developments, the exclusion of women from acting as pilots, gunners, or tank commanders has become harder to justify.

At the same time, the demand for able bodies in the age of the all-volunteer force created a need for women that eventually trumped the objections to women in the military. Women saw the armed forces as a good, stable job opportunity, where they could obtain skills and preparation and find an outlet for talents not always used in other jobs. As the percentage of women in the all-volunteer force grew, the military began more closely to resemble the general society, and as with the integration of African Americans, the fact that the public saw the military as a microcosm of the society at large played a role in generating support for it.

Finally, during the scandals of the 1990s, the public impression was that the military reacted quickly and swiftly to allegations of sexual harassment. That was not necessarily the way the media covered those stories. The public impression that the military was making a good-faith effort may not always have accurately reflected military attitudes. Still, in its responses to the Aberdeen and Tailhook incidents, the military seemed to have clear rules and effective ways to enforce those rules. Laws about sexual harassment and even assault in society in general are often ambiguous, and people may take comfort in the thought that in the military at least the rules are clear-cut, and discipline is swift and unequivocal. At a time when people confess to feeling that no moral codes unite Americans, the sense that the military has moral codes about sex may lead Americans to have more confidence in the military, even when they feel that military codes are unfair or overly harsh. In that respect, the military has been a litmus test against which the rest of society can measure itself, and the military has earned a reputation as the one government institution that can and does accomplish its goals competently.

The American public seems to embrace the professionalism the armed forces have shown in addressing issues of drug abuse, race, and gender integration. The actions taken by the military to deal with those problems have demonstrated its ability to adjust to changing American social values, while maintaining its effectiveness and integrity as a professional fighting force.

Politics and the Military

There is an irony in the fact that the military, which ranks as one of the more conservative institutions, has done yeoman work in dealing with what are typically thought of as "liberal" issues such as race and gender. One result of that, however, is that the military has become more intimately involved in nonmilitary political debates over those same issues. That in turn has blurred the traditional walls between civilian and military spheres of action. Noting that development, some scholars have expressed concern that increasing participation and influence by the armed forces in politics and policymaking could threaten military professionalism and ultimately lead to a decline in public support.

In recent years the military has been seen by some as taking a more active role in policymaking (especially in dictating foreign policy) and in participating in politics. There is also a sense that a growing gap exists between the military and society and that as a result tensions between civilian policymakers and the military will increase over the coming years. Indeed, during the Clinton administration, the military command was unusually vocal about its discomfort with the civilian commanders. As military leaders became less deferential toward elected and appointed officials, civil-military relations became strained. At the beginning of 2001 there was some indication, at least judging from the rhetoric, that the new Bush administration recognizes that breach. The Bush team, which includes former Pentagon officials such as Richard Cheney, Donald Rumsfeld, and Colin Powell, made it a priority to restore military confidence in the civilian authorities. How that will affect public confidence in military authorities remains an open question.

Civil-Military Tensions. One of Clinton's first acts as president was to attempt to rescind the military's ban on gay soldiers. Greeted with the nearly unanimous opposition of the senior officers and of the highly regarded Colin Powell, Clinton backtracked in the first months of 1993. That led to more than six months of congressional and military hearings on the issue, and with each month relations between the president and the armed forces deteriorated. It also undercut the president's authority in Congress. Article 1, section 8, of the U.S. Constitution gives Congress authority to regulate the military.

General Colin Powell's outspoken criticism of the proposed executive order lifting restrictions on gays in the military was part of a general tendency by Powell to insert himself into the political process. With few notable exceptions, such as Douglas MacArthur's defiance of the Truman administration in 1950 and 1951, military leaders had rarely given public expression to their disagreements with civilian commanders. That was seen as an act of insubordination. But in 1993 Powell published several pieces in *Foreign Affairs* laying out his vision of military strategy. The provisos he suggested, if incorporated into policy, would have significantly restricted the ability of civilian officials to use military force abroad. Powell's activist presence was taken by several commentators as representative of a general crisis in civil-military relations, with the balance of power swinging dangerously away from the civilians.[41]

Upon Powell's retirement, his public approval ratings were immensely high, and well into 1996 he was the presumptive favorite to win the presidential election should he have chosen to run. To the degree that people gave the issue of civil-military relations any thought, they seemed to favor Powell's perspective on the proper role and use of the armed forces over Clinton's. A number of observers viewed that fact with alarm, but it is not clear whether the public preference for Powell over Clinton, at least on military matters, signified any real shift in preferences for military over civilian control. In short, while Powell's popularity was yet another reason for public confidence in the military to increase, it does not follow that public confidence in civilian government has thereby suffered. Still, with Powell's appointment as secretary of state in 2001, it may be that the balance is shifting toward the military.

Political Activity in the Military. In recent years, as public confidence in the military has risen, a number of observers have pointed to what they believe is a dangerous trend that will in time undermine not only public confidence but also the military's ability to provide for American security.

In his writing on the military, Thomas Ricks, a former *Wall Street Journal* reporter now with the *Washington Post,* has documented a "widening gap" between civilian and military culture. The most significant manifestation of that gap, according to Ricks, is the ideological identification of military personnel relative to the identification of the population as a whole. Morris Janowitz, in his seminal study of the military in the 1970s, found that military officers tended to shy away from clear allegiances to one political party or ideology. If they leaned in any one direction, Janowitz said, it was toward the more liberal end of the spectrum. Not so today, argues Ricks.[42]

In surveys conducted by the services, and particularly those surveys conducted by the Foreign Policy Leadership Project, which included several hundred military officers from the Pentagon and various war colleges, Ricks discovered a pattern of increasing conservatism among officers relative to the centrism of the general population. "The military," wrote Ricks, "appears to be becoming politically less representative of society, with a long-term downward trend in the number of officers willing to identify themselves as liberal. Open identification with the Republican Party is becoming the norm."

In an opinion piece in the *Boston Globe*, James Carroll wrote that the heavy identification of military officers with the Republican Party threatens the integrity of the military as a nonpolitical guardian of American society.[43] Former military officers such as Bernard Trainor and Andrew Bacevich have spoken of their concern that today's officers are increasingly disenchanted with the society that they are supposed to serve.

A recent set of papers prepared at Duke University under the auspices of the Triangle Institute for Security Studies documents the civil-military gap.[44] Those studies deconstruct the concept of "trust" and find consistently lower trust among nonveterans. Important for recruiting, civilian elites who never served in the military are not supportive of their children's ever serving in the armed forces. In a 1999 survey, 22 percent of nonveteran civilian elites strongly agreed with the statement "I would be disappointed if a child of mine joined the military." The percentages "strongly agreeing" among active-duty military and civilian elites who *had* served in the military were 6.3 and 6.4 percent, respectively.[45] With respect to recruiting, the civilian-military gap seems to persist long after one's enlistment ends.

Expressions of disgust with lax morality in civilian society seem to be common in contemporary military culture. The degree to which Washington in the 1990s was consumed with details of presidential affairs and assorted misdoings served as a reminder to conservative officers that civilian society is morally rudderless and that only the military has preserved a sense of right and wrong, vital and trivial, moral and immoral. Yet, others argue, the surveys do not demonstrate such clear-cut trends, and finding anecdotal evidence that points in other directions is relatively easy.

According to political scientist Ole Holsti, some data support Ricks's contention that the military is more conservative on foreign policy and economic issues, but Holsti has questioned whether that tendency has become substantially more pronounced in the past few years. In addition, while Holsti has agreed that in several areas military leaders are more conservative than civilian leaders, he also has found areas where views are roughly parallel. Military officers believe, not surprisingly, in higher levels of military spending and lower levels of welfare spending, including Social Security and health care. But on issues such as crime, research money, education, and mass transit, civilian and military leaders are essentially in sync.[46]

Juxtaposed to Holsti's caveats is a set of anecdotal and not-so-anecdotal evidence. During the uncertain weeks following election day 2000, America waited for the returns from Florida's absentee ballots, which, we were assured by television commentators, would come mostly from U.S. military personnel stationed overseas and would heavily favor the Republican ticket of Bush-Cheney. That is precisely what happened, as the thousands of absentee ballots did indeed break Republican.

In addition to signaling the conservative ideological shift of the armed forces, officer voting behavior reveals that military professionals are becoming more active in politics. In *Making the Corps,* Ricks reported that since 1992 military personnel have voted in greater percentages than the general population. "This change is all the more striking," wrote Ricks, "because, while conservatism has long been present in the American military, political involvement is something of an anomaly."[47] Historically, soldiers have avoided political affiliation and have chosen to identify themselves as military professionals and not as Democrats or Republicans.[48]

Again, what are the consequences for public confidence? Traditionally, the public has viewed the military as a nonpoliticized institution. Samuel Huntington, one of the doyens of the study of civil-military relations, warned that the political participation of officers threatens professionalism by "dividing the profession against itself, and substituting extraneous values for professional values."[49] As public confidence in government institutions declines while it increases for the military, it becomes more apparent that people continue to separate the military profession from politics. But if political participation by the military increases to the extent that the public begins to view the armed forces as a politically "driven" organization, then public confidence in the institution could decline, as it has for other political institutions.

Most of the recent scholarship on the civil-military "gap" has focused on documenting its existence, not on explaining the source. Certainly, as David Segal, Peter Feaver, and others have noted, the advent of the all-volunteer force is a likely cause. We believe that the current conservative impulses of officers are another legacy of the Vietnam War, though an indirect one. In response to student protests, ROTC programs were closed down in the 1960s at campuses with more liberal students, such as Harvard and the University of Wisconsin. Those programs remain closed today and truncate the supply of potential officers who may be enticed to join after already committing to a school. At the same time, more traditionally conservative universities, such as the University of Virginia, retained ROTC programs in the 1960s and remain an important source of new recruits. In short, as a result of the Vietnam War, some of the roads that liberals might have taken into the military were closed off.

The debate over politicization and separation comes down to the question whether ideological identification really matters in terms of the military's ability to fulfill its role and in terms of public confidence in its ability to do so. It may be that military officers are disenchanted with the values they see as prevalent in the larger society, but there is as yet little indication that they are any less committed to protecting and serving that larger society. What is more, the gap between the military and civilians is most noticeable not between the general society and military culture, but between military officers and civilian leaders. Although Ricks and others have noted that this gap predates the election of President Clinton in 1993, it is hard not to wonder to what extent the clear cultural differences between the Clinton White House and the Pentagon heightened and sharpened the gap. It is equally hard not to wonder how much that gap will narrow in the far more military-friendly administration of George W. Bush.

Nonetheless, if the politicization of the military does lead to the erosion of the public confidence in the military, that could be damaging to military effectiveness. The waning years and immediate aftermath of the Vietnam War showed that more than a loose relationship exists between public approval and military morale, and military morale connects directly to military effectiveness. No matter how one looks at it, the civil-military gap opens the door to a host of issues.

Influence of Military Culture in Policymaking. Interestingly, as the political and ideological gap between civilians and the armed forces has seemingly increased, civilian policymaking appears to be ever more influenced by military culture. The phenomenon is not new. For over half a century the American way of life has blended in more and more with that of the military. A 1993 article in *Defense Monitor* traced the historical development of military influence in American society. In the piece the authors stated that the military draft played a major role in bringing American society closer to military culture:

> By the end of [World War II] 12 million Americans had become familiar with military organizations, values and methods of control and activity. Another 13 million Americans, although not as closely regimented, churned out weapons and war material from the centrally controlled and regulated military industries. These 25 million were almost one-fourth of the entire American population over 14 years of age.[50]

In previous eras of American history, the United States had demobilized at the conclusion of a war. While that process began in 1945, the cold war again saw the rise of the military's influence in Washington. The focus on international security also entailed a focus on defense. A National Security Council was created, as was the Defense Department, which brought the hitherto disparate services together in one mammoth organization.

In the heated and uncertain atmosphere of the cold war, policymakers began to seek out military solutions to a variety of policy problems, both diplomatic and domestic. True, that militarization was most evident in foreign policy, where successive administrations used the threat of nuclear weapons and a system of military alliances to try to contain the Soviet Union.[51] A side effect of the long struggle with the Soviet Union was that policymakers began applying military language and methods to domestic problems. Major domestic policy efforts were framed to the American public as "wars," such as the "war on poverty" and later the "war on drugs." Politicians also spoke of trade wars with other nations.[52] In short, American domestic policymaking took on the rhetoric of military conflict.

Not only were policy issues framed in military terms, but they were also addressed in a manner that resembled large, centrally organized and funded military campaigns. Congress created the vast network of interstate highways under legislation called the National Defense Highway Act. The shock of the Soviet Sputnik satellite in 1958 justified overdue education reform, which in the spirit of the times was called the National Defense Education Act.[53]

Although the cold war has come to an end, elements of military culture remain actively part of our policy toward domestic problems. Police SWAT teams use military tactics and equipment in dealing with crime, and even the criminal justice system has begun attempting to reform some criminals by putting them through "boot camps," which are modeled after basic military training programs.

Among children of the Baby Boomers, even military clothing has been in fashion throughout the 1990s, with young women as likely as young men to wear combat boots and fatigues.

Precisely how the militarization of government and of aspects of larger culture affects public attitudes toward the military is difficult to say. In the cultural realm especially, most people are probably not attuned to that militarization. The climate of comfort with military imagery and military organization certainly does no harm to the military's image, and it may make people more comfortable with the military than might otherwise have been the case.

The military's *performance* and the evidence of the military's *professionalism* have helped shape public attitudes and generated public confidence. The public is aware of military performance and professionalism only because the services have made assiduous efforts to get the word out. To some degree, the image of the military as an organization that has overcome the problems of drugs, race, and gender integration and that supports traditional values is just that: an image. Even the image of the military as an unerring fighting force has overlooked the very real problems that plagued the missions in Grenada, Somalia, and Haiti. This is not to say that it is an inaccurate portrait. It is an image carefully and deliberately promoted by the military, in its efforts to recruit soldiers and in its continuing attempt to convince Congress to maintain high levels of spending. The image of the military as a clean-cut bastion of respect for the law and traditional values did not suffuse the culture by mystery or chance. That image was carefully constructed by the military in the wake of the Vietnam War and then brilliantly exported by an expensive and polished series of advertising and marketing campaigns. Those were yet another ingredient in the positive impression most Americans hold of the U.S. armed forces.

5

Persuasion

"Be All That You Can Be!" blasted television commercials aired throughout the country in 1981. The Army, concerned that it would not be able to meet enlistment goals, decided to implement a large-scale, costly, and polished marketing campaign. Nineteen seventy-nine had not been a good year for Army recruiting, and for the third straight year, the Army failed to meet its recruiting goals.

With the end of conscription in 1973, the military had to change the way it approached recruitment. That effort would begin by changing the negative picture the public had of the military after the Vietnam conflict. In 1969 President Nixon's Commission on an All-Volunteer Force concluded: "We unanimously believe that the nation's interests will be better served by an all-volunteer force. . . . We have satisfied ourselves that a volunteer force will not jeopardize national security, and we believe it will have a beneficial effect on the military as well as the rest of our society."[1] One of the most important psychological effects of ending the draft was that in essence it removed the military as a threat to the American public. As long as young men feared being drafted to fight a war that they did not understand or support, they viewed the military not as the defender of domestic security but as an ever present danger to their very lives. Fighting in Vietnam could kill one, so being drafted was perceived as a direct threat to life and livelihood.[2] As long as the armed forces were seen in that way and not as a defender of American values and freedoms, the military's ability to command resources and men and to mobilize them effectively was hampered.

The Gates Commission recommending the formation of the

all-volunteer force had suggested that "funds be made available . . . to assess the cost-effectiveness of paid radio and television advertising." In a ten-week period in 1971, the Army spent $10 million doing just that, and it found that enlistments would go up relative to how many spots were aired. The initial slogans were "Today's Army Wants You to Join," followed by "Join the People Who've Joined the Army." Those ad campaigns held out the promise that joining the Army was an act of public service and that once there, soldiers could be proud to work with each other. Through 1976, Army recruiting was quite successful.[3] But then Congress decreased total defense spending and with that cut funds appropriated for advertising. Congress also pressured the Army and the Pentagon not to glamorize the military in those spots that continued to be aired. As a result, enlistments dropped, and recruitment goals were not met.

The Army in particular suffered from the strong antiwar sentiment during those years, and the predisposition of the public to blame the Army for failure in Vietnam hampered the efforts of the service to put a positive spin on a military career. In 1980 in a survey of more than 900,000 males aged sixteen to twenty-one, 75 percent said that they probably would not or definitely would not consider serving in the military, and those that would preferred the Air Force or the Navy.[4] Those years coincided with the drop-off in the qualifications of recruits. By 1980, although the Army was nearly meeting its recruitment targets, fewer enlistees were high school graduates, and few were anywhere near the top of the labor pool in terms of skills.[5]

Paid Advertising

The Army entered the 1980s confronting a troubling demographic development. The young male population was declining, and young men evinced a disinclination to enlist. The Army's primary recruiting challenge was to convince seventeen- to nineteen-year-olds to take a break between high school and college and to join the Army. Most young people expressed the desire to go to college, so the Army needed to accommodate that aspiration. Determined to solve its recruitment quandary, the Army started to use one of the primary tools of marketers: focus groups. The focus groups uncovered the disturbing but hardly surprising truth that the Army suffered from an extremely negative image. Young people recognized what the Army offered in terms of skills, but juxtaposed to the negative images, what the Army offered was not a sufficient inducement. So the Army, in the words of the man who helped coordinate its marketing campaign, did what any faltering company does. It attempted to "reposition its products."[6]

After another extensive round of focus groups and market research, the Army concluded that the biggest draw for young people would be technology. The more the Army was seen as a high-tech environment of skilled professionals, the greater its appeal would be. In addition, the more funds the Army could contribute to an enlistee's college education, the more likely high school seniors would be to join.

In response to focus groups and market testing, the Army was able to convince the Pentagon to allocate funds that would essentially constitute a new GI bill for college education. Advances in weapons systems made it necessary for personnel of the Army to have the skills to operate the new technology effectively, and the college GI bill created an incentive to attract skilled high school graduates.

The Army's first emphasis on the college fund ran as a major television campaign in 1981, and it proved successful in raising enlistments without cutting into the Navy or Air Force enlistments. The Army's internal organization, however, created problems. Instead of one centralized advertising program, the Army had fifteen different programs managed by five separate organizations, although the Recruiting Command had the primary responsibility and the largest share of resources.[7] In addition, some senior officers objected to the whole notion of marketing the Army as if it were a bar of soap. Eventually, those internal obstacles were overcome, and that paved the way for the "Be All That You Can Be!" campaign.

A leading Madison Avenue advertiser, N. W. Ayer, wrote the jingle and the many different text versions of the campaign.

Although the marketing program also used direct mail and print advertising, television was the linchpin. Images of young men, and occasionally women, engaged in exciting, high-tech activities like flying helicopters or practicing infrared night missions, were combined with promises of further education both within the Army and subsequently in college. Half a million bumper stickers were printed, and "Be All That You Can Be!" music was distributed to 16,000 high school band directors.[8]

The campaign helped reverse the image of the Army. The slogan became as recognizable as that for McDonald's Big Mac. The Army success at "branding" its slogan spurred the other services to improve their advertising, and the Marine Corps came up with "The Few, the Proud, the Marines," which lasted through the 1990s. The Army's campaign improved both the number and the quality of recruits, as judged from high school ranking and scores on the Armed Forces Qualification Test. Nineteen eighty-four was the best year for Army recruiting. Ninety percent were high school graduates and 63 percent scored above average on the qualification test.[9] Given that television is the primary way most Americans receive information about the world, the Army's adroit use of advertising must count as a major factor in changing the image of the military in American society.

In the late 1980s and 1990s, the Marines were at least as successful in marketing their warrior image. In a series of startling graphic-based ads, the Marines sold themselves with images of a young man jousting with medieval knights on a high-tech chessboard. Toward the end of the 1990s and into the early 2000s, the Marines used even more fantastical imagery meant to evoke a high-end computer game. Those spots were shown in movie theaters and aired at the same time as previews for coming Hollywood blockbusters. The Navy has also sold itself using imagery derived from video games. All the services have made use of the most refined advertising and market testing techniques that Madison Avenue has to offer. Judging from recruitment response and the recognizability of the slogans, those advertising campaigns have been an unqualified success in associating the military with images of skilled soldiers preparing for college while defending their country in exciting, glamorous, and adventuresome ways.

Military advertising has tended to focus on training, good pay, and good benefits. Not surprisingly then, a 1998 Army survey of 9,000 recent recruits found 80 percent citing "good benefits" as an important or extremely important reason for joining. Seventy-eight percent cited good pay. Conspicuously lower in ranking, service to the country was cited by 50 percent of new recruits as a reason for joining the army.[10] Patriotism may be undermarketed.[11] In fact, in late 2000, the Army replaced its "Be All That You Can Be" campaign with a new slogan. The old one had more than served its purpose, but even the best ad campaigns eventually lose their effectiveness. With much fanfare, the Army unveiled its new slogan, "An Army of One." Critics were quick to point out the inherent individualism, even selfishness, in the idea. Having attracted the youth of the 1980s with promises of self-improvement, the Army of the new millennium hopes to attract the next generation with the promise of individual glory.

Free Advertising

In the 1990s, while the armed forces continued to spend millions of dollars on television commercials, some of their best advertising came free. The military victories in Panama, Iraq, and most recently in Kosovo have been broadcast to millions of Americans on prime-time network television. For several weeks during those conflicts, the American public saw well-organized press briefings that featured video images of U.S. armed forces in combat. Constant images of military warships, aircraft, and soldiers convincingly defeating the enemy enhanced the public's perception of the military and improved the relationship between the media and the armed forces.

Mutual distrust characterized the relationship between the armed forces and the media throughout the cold war and into the Vietnam conflict. But the military did a better job at "packaging" the news for the media in the 1990s. It also did a better job controlling what journalists saw and to whom they could talk. The low point of military-media relations came during the Vietnam War when a Pentagon made paranoid by the hostile media tried to cover up embarrassing military operations.[12]

In the 1980s, however, the military began to improve its relations with the media and to use news coverage of military operations to enhance the public image of the armed forces. Indeed, in recent years the armed forces have often been the center of media attention. In large part that attention has kept the military in the forefront of American life and also helped to persuade young men and women to enlist.

The media coverage of the Gulf War provides a good example of the military benefiting as a result of extensive press coverage. Part of that coverage involved the reporting of the very small number of casualties of U.S. forces involved in the conflict. That was a sharp contrast to the images of dead and wounded soldiers seen by Americans daily during the Vietnam War. In his study of recruiting challenges, Robert Goldich assessed the impact of the press coverage of the Gulf War on individuals thinking of enlisting in the armed forces. "Desert Storm," wrote Goldich, "clearly provides an incentive to volunteer: If you go to war, you may win big and probably won't get killed or even wounded."[13]

Certainly, not all press coverage has been favorable to the military: Tailhook, Aberdeen, the disappearance of an A-10 aircraft in the Rocky Mountains, and, most damaging of all, the Pentagon's continued mishandling of the "Gulf War Syndrome."[14] Some of those episodes represented the normal crises and problems that confront a world of 1.5 million soldiers, thousands of missions and bases, and inevitable human errors. But they become magnified in a media world that has made the military a recurring story. If an A-10 had disappeared in the mid-1960s, for example, there likely would have been little public discussion. In the 1990s the military was under constant press scrutiny, yet negative stories about the military do not seem to have made a substantial dent in public confidence.

In addition to nurturing more positive relations with the media, the services have also developed a symbiotic relationship with Hollywood in the age of the action blockbuster. A number of movies, from *Top Gun* to *The Hunt for Red October, Iron Eagle III,* and most recently, *Saving Private Ryan,* have presented the military as a universe of competitive, competent, and dynamic individuals. Some of those movies benefited from the active cooperation of the services in providing movie studios with access to ships, planes, guns, and personnel as extras. Television shows such as *J.A.G.* have also enjoyed the full cooperation of the services, and that has also burnished their image. Aided by the saturation of positive images in movies and on television, the public profile of the military changed about as much as one could imagine between the mid-1970s and the late 1980s.

Hollywood has long had a comfortable relationship with the Pentagon, and the Pentagon indirectly subsidized World War II movies. The Pentagon began working with the entertainment industry very actively in the late 1970s. Today, "[a] filmmaker who wishes to make use of the military's tanks, aircraft carriers, jet fighters, or nuclear submarines in a film or who wants to shoot on bases or other military installations must first submit his or her screenplay to the Pentagon for approval."[15] The Army even publishes a manual, A *Producer's Guide to U.S. Army Cooperation with the Entertainment Industry,* which lays out ground rules for setting the right tone in a script. As reported by David Robb, the Pentagon's officials in charge of working with Hollywood are plain about the goals of cooperating with producers. One Pentagon memo to the producers of the 1994 movie *Clear and Present Danger* noted, "[M]ilitary depictions have become more of a 'commercial' for us."[16] Table 5-1 shows the selection of movies accepted and rejected for Pentagon subsidies since 1970.

The events of September 11 had a huge impact on the fiction and nonfiction media, with initial around-the-clock coverage of events as they unfolded first in the United States and then in Afghanistan. News coverage of the operation in Afghanistan was generally favorable. At the movies, the initial postponement of films with overwhelming violence and destruction gave way to a trend toward films involving war and espionage with positive portrayals

Table 5-1 Selection of Movies Accepted and Rejected for Pentagon Subsidies

Approved	Year	Not Approved
The Sum of All Fears[a] (Paramount)	2002	
Behind Enemy Lines[a] (20th Cent. Fox)	2001	
Pearl Harbor[a] (Buena Vista)		
The Perfect Storm[a] (Warner Bros.)	2000	*Space Cowboys* (Warner Bros.)
Random Hearts (Columbia)	1999	*The General's Daughter* (Paramount)
	1998	*Saving Private Ryan* (DreamWorks)
Armageddon[a] (Touchstone)		*Thin Red Line* (20th Century Fox)
Air Force One[a] (Columbia)	1997	*G.I. Jane*[a] (Buena Vista)
Executive Decision (Warner Bros.)	1996	*Broken Arrow* (20th Century Fox)
Fly Away Home (TriStar)		*Independence Day*[a] (20th Century Fox)
The American President (Columbia)	1995	*Crimson Tide* (Buena Vista)
Clear and Present Danger[a] (Paramount)	1994	*Forrest Gump* (Paramount)
A Few Good Men[a] (Columbia)	1992	*Iron Eagle III* (New Line)
Flight of the Intruder (Paramount)	1991	*For the Boys* (20th Century Fox)
The Hunt for Red October (Paramount)	1990	*Die Hard 2* (20th Century Fox)
	1989	*Born on the 4th of July* (Universal)
Biloxi Blues (Universal)	1988	
Hamburger Hill (Paramount)	1987	*Full Metal Jacket* (Warner Bros.)
Top Gun[a] (Paramount)	1986	*Platoon* (Orion)
Firefox (Warner Bros.)	1982	*An Officer and a Gentleman* (Paramount)
Stripes (Columbia)	1981	
The Great Santini (Orion)	1979	*Apocalypse Now* (United Artists)
Midway (Universal)	1976	
Patton (20th Century Fox)	1970	*Catch-22* (Paramount)

a. Script changes required.
Source: Robb (2001).

of the men and women responsible for defending the country. *Black Hawk Down* and *Windtalkers* portrayed the heroism of soldiers past and present, while the movie version of Tom Clancy's novel *The Sum of All Fears* allowed the Central Intelligence Agency to get in on the act. The production staff for *The Sum of All Fears* received technical assistance from the military and the CIA as well as access to some restricted parts of CIA headquarters and the use of enough military hardware and personnel to make the "celluloid equivalent of a small nation's armed forces."[17] If that recent trend is any indication, cooperation between Hollywood and the Pentagon will be a mainstay of the post–September 11 media landscape and is likely to influence young moviegoers nationwide for years to come.

The shift in public attitudes coincided with rising defense budgets, Reagan's unabashed throwback patriotism, and a series of military successes in Grenada, Panama, and the Gulf. It may be that without those factors, the turnaround in image would not have been accomplished so easily. Yet, even by 1982, the military's image was showing startling improvement, and that predated the string of military successes.

The inability of recent negative press accounts to cause a drop in public confidence in the military should give us some pause before we ascribe the rise in public confidence in the 1980s to good public relations. It may also be that the positive effects of advertising and movies that continue to portray the military in a positive light have a greater influence on public attitudes than the press, which itself is held in very low public esteem. Therefore, the efforts put forth by the armed forces to improve relations with the media and Hollywood, as well as the multimillion-dollar advertising campaigns, must be treated as a vital link in the shift in public attitudes toward the military.

Young people in particular seem to have responded favorably to free and paid advertising. While the armed forces have tried to raise their profile for myriad reasons, recruitment remains the primary motivation and the primary rationale for spending money on advertising and on Hollywood outreach. In that sense, how men and women in their late teens and early twenties respond to the military matters more than how their parents respond.

It is well known that long lines formed at Navy recruiting offices the day after *Top Gun* premiered, but the effects of "persuasion" are constant and persuasive among children of the Baby Boomers. Junior high school students receive free book covers with colored glossy pictures of planes and tanks. Some of the most popular video games feature military themes and make adolescents protagonists in combat and peacekeeping. The more negative military images an adolescent is exposed to, the lower one's confidence in the armed forces. The reverse is also true, and "persuasion" has been an effective tool for getting the good word out to potential recruits.

6

Generations and Marketing for the Twenty-first Century

Public confidence in the military today is the envy of most government agencies. Unlike a generation ago, the military places higher in polls than do universities (and professors), hospitals (and doctors), and churches (and clergy). This is an impressive accomplishment, and there are many contributing factors, including internal reforms that increased the probability of battlefield successes, an apparent ability to deal effectively with problems that plague society (especially drugs and racial integration), and the successful marketing of the military to potential recruits.

To those of us in colleges, today's military recruiting strategies echo what universities do to attract students. If Harvard University failed to recruit a large and high-quality class for even one year, the institution would be badly degraded. Two or three years of bad recruiting for most universities could mean the end.

Since the American people pay for the U.S. armed forces, the military needs to remain ever vigilant to maintain public confidence. Public confidence translates into support within Congress. Support in Congress need not come from veterans, and the military's braying about a lack of veterans among legislators and staffers seems silly. While older veterans show more confidence in the military than one finds among nonveterans, Vietnam-era veterans are significantly less supportive of the military.

The python of time is swallowing the Great Depression generation, and along with it that generation's high support for the military. Public confidence in the military has gone up despite that—partly because the youngest generation is replacing the older one. In the middle of their life cycle, Baby Boomers are taking the reins of power. Accordingly, the military needs to maintain a strong program of persuasion—coupled with performance and professionalism—aimed at future recruits.

With the strong economy and the expansion of student loans to vocational schools, the military is having a more difficult time enlisting young men and women. We have already noted the irony that nineteen- to twenty-year-olds have the highest confidence in the military, yet today's high school seniors are much less willing to join the armed forces than their counterparts a decade ago. For recruiting, the impact of good public relations has been difficult to discern, especially in the late 1990s.

Yet persuasion—or marketing the military—has ramifications far beyond recruitment and retention. "Be All That You Can Be!" has been an anthem for millions of young men and women who never considered joining the armed forces, but who are broadly supportive in ways their Vietnam War–era parents could scarcely imagine. Obviously, the Army hopes that the "Army of One" campaign will at least match the appeal of "Be All That You Can Be!"

History is not linear; it moves in cycles, and this may well be a golden era of public support for the military. The public, though, may be fickle (witness the dramatic drop in confidence among black high school seniors during and after the Gulf War). One can easily imagine public confidence in the military falling had the war in Kosovo not turned out well. The war on terrorism presents a new set of challenges for the U.S. military, and while the country seems to be indulgent in allowing both the military and the political leadership to conduct the war as they see fit, that extra wartime leeway will eventually wear off.

For the moment, it appears that the public is more willing to think badly of civilian government than it is to distrust the military. As events in Somalia in 1993 demonstrated, the public has little trouble believing that civilian officials are prone to errors and misjudgments. Given a choice between blaming the military and blaming the government, people are more likely to blame the government.

The Bush-Cheney administration ran on a platform that placed the health of the armed forces at the center of policy concerns. Angered by the dissension of the Clinton years, and by what they took to be the neglect of the military by the Baby Boomers of the Clinton White House, Bush and Cheney promised to restore military budgets and revive sagging morale. They recognize that the military needs regular injections of public enthusiasm to thrive. Cheney and Powell know that public confidence and enthusiasm for the military cannot be taken for granted. And they realize that the military can only derive so much benefit from negative images of civilian Washington.

The image of the military as an efficient, skilled organization was contrasted throughout the 1980s and 1990s in the public mind by an image of Washington as a pit of corruption and inefficiency. Two decades ago, after the failed rescue attempt of the hostages in Tehran, people were far more willing to see the military as inept. Throughout the Clinton years, they were likely to believe that the military is capable but that it is often undermined by the fecklessness of politicians. But with the end of the Clinton administration, the armed forces are no longer able to derive any benefit from that contrast. Even before September 11, President Bush seemed determined to use that reading of the Clinton years to generate higher military budgets.

It will take more than an image of the military as efficient and skilled to continue attracting talented young men and women. Just as the military reinvented its public image in the 1980s and 1990s, it needs to continue such reinvention in the years ahead. Such reinvention will require careful attention to the data on public confidence that we analyzed above. It will require even more awareness of what Gen Xers and what the next generation of young people are looking for in life. Convincing them to enlist will be no easy task, and ironically, it may be made even harder in the next years. Individuals such as Powell who have a marked disinclination to use force abroad also lead the Bush administration, the most military-friendly administration since Reagan. We have seen, however, that successful use of force abroad has been one of the primary draws of the military. How the military will demonstrate its ability in a time when it is hardly deployed is a conundrum that the service chiefs will have to grapple with in a Bush administration.

The war on terrorism will surely lead to increased deployment, yet the nature of fighting terrorists presents a unique challenge to the armed forces. Without targets more concrete than a "terrorist infrastructure" comprising e-mail and Web sites as much as bunkers and caves, it will be difficult to measure progress. Indeed, successes in the war on terrorism are often hidden from public view, because success is the avoidance of an attack that one would otherwise not know might occur. How is that to be covered on television? A single failure—just one successful attack on American soil, no matter how much infrastructure was destroyed or how many terrorists were previously eliminated—could blind Americans from seeing the espionage victories that preceded the terrorist act.

It is not that military leaders are unaware that public support and confidence depend in part on the actual record. That is part of the problem. On the one hand, the more the military succeeds, the more it will be perceived as a success. But the obverse is also true, and that may help explain why military officials have become noticeably reluctant to deploy force. Not only are they unwilling to risk lives unless the reasons are overwhelmingly important, but they do not willingly embrace missions where the odds of success are not overwhelmingly on their side. Public confidence in the military may, therefore, have the unintended consequence of leading to fewer military operations rather than more.

Furthermore, public confidence in the military seems confined to the military acting in its proper sphere. No indication exists that people are willing to entrust governance to the military, nor is there any reason to suppose that the public would welcome military involvement in civilian matters such as health care or Social Security or even debates on the size of the military budget. Citizen confidence in the military appears to be confined to confidence in the military's ability to perform military tasks. It does not entail a desire that the role of the military in civilian governance be expanded. In that respect, there should be little concern that declining respect for the federal government combined with substantial respect for the military could lead to a dangerous imbalance in civil-military authority.

While a Bush administration may be more aggressive in authorizing the use of force, the military will, in all likelihood, continue to be deployed for numerous "nonlethal" missions. In the twenty-first century, the American military is preparing to do things that the cold war military did not: supplying disaster relief, peacekeeping, policing, rescue missions, counterterrorism, smoothing the transition to civilian rule in newly formed countries, and maintaining a forward presence not in preparation for war but to preserve the balance in regions such as the Far East and the Persian Gulf. Such nontraditional roles have not replaced the core mission of the armed forces. The military is still expected to manage the U.S. nuclear arsenal and still expected to be able to fight major, conventional wars. With each new mission that the military acquires, it also acquires potential liabilities and more possibility for failure. And if several missions were to go awry, even low-level, nonlethal missions such as disaster relief, public confidence might quickly erode.

For an institution to command public confidence, it needs to be seen as possessing integrity. That is, its mission needs to be respected, and people have to believe that its leaders are dedicated to the mission above all. Furthermore, institutions need to be seen addressing problems squarely and honorably. The fact that the military was plagued by problems of race and gender, and to some degree is still trying to grapple with a racially and gender integrated fighting force, is less troublesome to the public because the military seems to be addressing those problems with integrity.

Confidence in institutions takes years to build but far less time to erode. For institutions as for buildings, it is easier to tear down than to construct. One reason that military leaders have been so "conservative" in the past decade is that they have been wary of jeopardizing public respect that had been so hard won.

Any institution can lose public confidence; that is easy. Restoring confidence is the real challenge. It is one that the military has met, and one that other government institutions ought to study and emulate.

Appendix

Multivariate Analysis of Confidence
in the Leaders of the Military

Because the outcome we are trying to understand takes on three possible outcomes ("a great deal," "some," and "hardly any" confidence), we employ an ordered probit technique in a pooled cross-section of the General Social Surveys spanning 1973 through 2000.

For our purposes, the relative sizes of the estimated coefficients are not so illuminating as whether a variable is statistically significant and whether the variable dampens or heightens confidence in the military.

Variable Measurements. "Black" is a 0,1 dummy variable. "Female" is a dummy variable. "Education" equals the number of years of education. "Unemployed" is a dummy variable, as is "married." "Age" is in years. The generational dummy variables represent the generational categories shown in table 2-1. "Conservatism" is along a seven-point scale with self-identified "very liberal" at 1 and "very conservative" at 7. "Ideological extremist" is 1 if conservatism equals 1 or 7. "Religious fundamentalist" is a dummy variable, and "hours TV daily" ranges from 0 to 7. "Success in year" is 1 for Grenada (1983), Panama (1989), Desert Storm (1991), and Haiti (1994). "Failure in year" is 1 for Desert One (1980), Beirut (1983), and Somalia (1992). Note that Baby Boomers are the excluded category for the generational dummy variables. We also used a few interactions for generations and found that Generation X blacks have less

Table A-1 Public Confidence in Leaders of the U.S. Military, Ordered Probit Estimate, Pooled Cross-Section, 1973–2000

	Coefficient	z	$P>|z|$
Demographics			
Black	−.063	−1.97	.049
Female	−.112	−6.01	.000
Education	−.142	−11.26	.000
Unemployed	−.094	−1.74	.082
Married	.051	2.63	.008
Age	.000	0.07	.941
Generations (Baby Boomers Excluded)			
Depression era	.216	3.58	.000
WWII and Korean War	.100	2.98	.003
Generation X	.154	3.87	.000
Gen X – black	−.312	3.36	.001
Millennial	.356	3.36	.001
Millennial – black	−.303	−1.22	.223
Political and Cultural Values			
Conservatism	.075	10.58	.000
Ideological extremist	−.135	−3.30	.001
Religious fundamentalist	.139	6.61	.000
Hours TV daily	.023	4.14	.000
Military Performance			
Success in year	.116	4.44	.000
Failure in year	−.163	−5.67	.000
Time Trend			
Year of survey	.006	3.37	.001
Ancillary Parameters			
Cut point 1	11.88	Number of obs. = 15,625	
Cut point 2	13.44	chi^2 (20) = 749.01	
		Prob. > chi^2 = .0000	

Source: NORC 1973–2000 Cumulative Survey.

confidence in the military than their nonwhite counterparts. That effect disappears for Millennial blacks.

Notes

Chapter 1: Public Trust

1. See Morin and Deane (2001). In the poll N = 1,215 adults nationwide.

2. See Nye, Zelikow, and King (1997).

3. These rallies can be short-lived. In August 1950, for example, 66 percent of respondents told the Gallup organization that the United States had not "made a mistake in going into the war in Korea." By June 1951 just 39 percent still said it was not a mistake. See Mueller (1973, table 3.1A). Compare Sobel (2001, 31).

4. See Sobel (2001, chap. 4); Mueller (1973).

5. See Lipset and Schneider (1983, 383).

6. See Inglehart (1997; 1999). In contrast, see Sobel (1999).

7. See H. Bray (2002).

8. See "Confidence in Institutions" (1995, 70–73).

9. For an overview of the Goldwater-Nichols Act, see Locher (1996, 10–16).

10. The question asked in 1973–1978, 1979–1980, 1982–1984, 1985–1991, 1993–1994, 1996, 1998, and 2000: "I am going to name some institutions in this country. As far as the people running these institutions are concerned, would you say you have a great deal of confidence, only some confidence, or hardly any confidence at all in them? Military."

11. See Hamilton (1998).

12. We have tried, in various ways, to measure "authoritarianism" among respondents, and while religious fundamentalism is sometimes treated as a proxy for authoritarianism, we do not embrace that interpretation here. For

now, at least, authoritarianism goes unexamined. For a full exploration, see Sobel (2000).

Chapter 2: The Generational Gulf

1. See Ricks (1997a, 32).
2. See Geisler (1999, 61).
3. See Davis and Smith (1999). Compare Mueller (1994).
4. See Strauss and Howe (1991); Howe and Strauss (2000).
5. See Rainer (1997); Zoba (1999); Barna (1995).
6. See McAllister (1999).
7. See Institute of Politics (2002).
8. See McClam (2001).
9. See Howe and Strauss (2000).
10. See Johnston, Bachman, and O'Malley (1998); Segal and Bachman (1994).
11. See Deputy Assistant Secretary of Defense (1999).

Chapter 3: Performance

1. See Summers (1982).
2. See McNamara (1995). See also Hendrickson (1996). On the degree to which the military deceived the public, see Summers (1982, 61–82).
3. See Mueller (1973); Wells (1994). On Vietnam as a general cause of declining confidence in government, see Orren (1997, 77–107).
4. How survey questions are worded matters. In the early 1970s, large differences existed in the percentage of respondents supporting "the military" and having confidence "in the people in charge of the military." Especially at the close of the Vietnam War, respondents associated "the people in charge" with civilians who were overseeing the military. See Segal and Blair (1976).
5. See "The NORC Series of Confidence in Leaders of National Institutions" (1997); "Confidence in Institutions" (1995, 70–73).
6. See Kitfield (1995; 1994, 1400); Timberg (1995); Harrison (1982).

7. See Baritz (1985).

8. See Ruane (1995); General John Shaud (U.S. Air Force), interview with Zachary Karabell, April 9, 1998.

9. Statistics about high school graduates and Trainor were quoted in Ricks (1997a, 22).

10. See Moskin (1992, 660ff.); Ricks (1997b); Huntington and Kohn (1994); Margerum (1983).

11. See Graf (1985). Meyer was quoted in Kitfield (1994, 1400). The statistics on drug use as of 1980 are from "Like Other Segments of Culture, Military Has Had to Come to Grips with Drug Abuse Problems" (1989, 2785).

12. See Sick (1985, 338–56).

13. General John Shaud (U.S. Air Force), interview with Zachary Karabell, April 9, 1998.

14. For Reagan and the military, see Cannon (1991).

15. Lieutenant Colonel William DeCamp (U.S. Marine Corps), interview with Zachary Karabell, April 9, 1998.

16. See Hart and Lind (1986); Summers (1982). For a history of John Boyd's maneuverability theory and the early origins of the reform movement, see Smith (1985, 33).

17. See Summers (1982, xiii).

18. For a critical analysis of Powell and the Goldwater-Nichols Act, see "Colin Powell as JCS Chairman: A Panel Discussion on American Civil-Military Relations" (1995). See also Weinberger (1990b); Crowe (1993); Haass (1994).

19. See Burrowes (1988); Treverton (1986); Shultz (1993, 326–29).

20. Buckley (1991); Gliboa (1995–1996); Woodward (1991, 54ff.).

21. See Patros (1993, 281).

22. See Mueller (1994).

23. See ibid., 161–63.

24. See Mueller (1973); Barnet (1990). On the "Vietnam syndrome," see Powell with Persico (1995); Trainor and Gordon (1995).

25. See Morganthau et al. (1991).

26. See Stevenson (1993, 138–54); Hirsch and Oakley (1995).

Chapter 4: Professionalism

1. See Comptroller General of the United States (1971); Helmer (1974, 71–91).

2. See Weinberger (1990b, 29).

3. See "Like Other Segments of Culture, Military Has Had to Come to Grips with Drug Abuse Problems" (1989, 2785).

4. See R. Bray (1992, 476–96).

5. See R. Bray (1999).

6. See Janowitz and Moskos (1974); Foner (1974, 211ff.); Westheider (1997, 94–115).

7. See Binkin and Eitelberg (1982, 41–43).

8. See Binkin (1984, 20–21).

9. See Binkin and Eitelberg (1982, 45–51).

10. See ibid., 92.

11. See Kageff and Laurence (1994).

12. See Bergmann (1996); Kahlenberg (1996).

13. See Butler (1980); Korb (1996); Mullen (1973, 64–95).

14. General John Galvin (U.S. Army), interview with Zachary Karabell, April 9, 1998.

15. See Moskos and Butler (1996, 35).

16. See ibid., 84–92; Dickerson (1997, 73).

17. See Segal and Bachman (1994, 156).

18. Quoted in Moskos and Butler (1996, 118).

19. See Klein (1995, 35). We should note that this interpretation is far from universally held. Peter Feaver cautions that some observers (especially Republicans) hold that Powell is evidence that one does not need affirmative action.

20. See Moskos and Butler (1996, 106).

21. Deputy Assistant Secretary of Defense (1999).

22. See Moskos (1998).

23. The amendment failed to be ratified by enough states.

24. See Holm (1992b); Korb (1996, 13–19); Miller (1998).

25. See U.S. Army (1982).

26. See Binkin and Bach (1977, 39–40).

27. See Elsthtain (1987, 241–45).

28. See M. Segal (1993, 81–93).

29. See Binkin and Bach (1977, 48–50).

30. See Korb (1996, 19).

31. See "Race, Sex, and Support for Women in the Military" (1992, 313–17).

32. See Binkin (1993, 54–57).

33. See U.S. Army (1982); M. Segal (1982).

34. See Holm (1992b, 290–303).

35. See Miller (1998, 33–64).

36. See Rayner (1997); Kitfield (1994).

37. See Franke (1997, 247–52); Schneider and Schneider (1988, 43–52, 137–80).

38. See Holm (1992a); Gutman (1997).

39. See "Misconduct in the Military" (1997); Goldberg (1997).

40. See "Sex and the Service" (1997, 5).

41. See Kohn (1994, 3–17); Luttwak (1994, 29–33).

42. See Ricks (1997b, 66–68); Janowitz (1995, passim). The most important work on military professionalism continues to be Huntington (1957).

43. See Carroll (2002).

44. See Feaver and Gelpi (1999); Gronke (1999).

45. See Gronke and Feaver (2001); Hendrickson (1988).

46. See Holsti (1998–1999). This article was originally prepared at Duke University as a response to Ricks. See also Johnson and Metz (1995).

47. See Ricks (1997a, 282).

48. See ibid., 284.

49. The Huntington quotation is from ibid., 282.

50. See Center for Defense Information (1993, 4).

51. See ibid., 5.

52. See ibid.

53. See ibid., 6.

Chapter 5: Persuasion

1. See Binkin and Eitelberg (1982, 39).

2. General John Shaud (U.S. Air Force) and General John Galvin (U.S. Army), interviews with Zachary Karabell, April 9, 1998.

3. Much of these data and analysis comes from Graf (1985). Graf was director of advertising and sales promotion, U.S. Army Recruiting Command, from 1980 to 1984.

4. See ibid., 11.

5. See Kageff and Laurence (1994).

6. See Graf (1985, 25).

7. See ibid., 36.

8. See ibid., 39–41.

9. On difficulties of interpreting those trends, see Kageff and Laurence (1994, 90).

10. See D. Segal (1999).

11. See Moskos (1988).

12. See Barnes (1996, 59).

13. See Goldich (1994, 122).

14. See Forster (1997, 15ff).

15. See Robb (2001, 136).

16. See ibid.

17. See Seelye (2002).

References

Baritz, Loren. 1985. *Backfire.* New York: Morrow.

Barna, George. 1995. *Generation Next.* Ventura, Calif.: Regal Books.

Barnes, Rudolph C., Jr. 1996. *Military Legitimacy: Might and Right in the New Millennium.* London: Frank Cass.

Barnet, Richard. 1990. *The Rockets' Red Glare: When America Goes to War.* New York: Simon and Schuster.

Bergmann, Barbara. 1996. *In Defense of Affirmative Action.* New York: Basic Books.

Binkin, Martin. 1984. *America's Volunteer Military: Progress and Prospects.* Washington, D.C.: Brookings Institution.

———. 1993. *Who Will Fight the Next War?* Washington, D.C.: Brookings Institution.

Binkin, Martin, and Shirley J. Bach. 1977. *Women and the Military.* Washington, D.C.: Brookings Institution.

Binkin, Martin, and Mark J. Eitelberg. 1982. *Blacks and the Military.* Washington, D.C.: Brookings Institution.

Bray, Hiawatha. 2002. "America's Army Set for Battle." *Boston Globe.* July 3.

Bray, Robert. 1992. "Progress toward Eliminating Drug and Alcohol Abuse among U.S. Soldiers." *Armed Forces and Society* 18 (4): 476–96.

———. 1999. "Highlights: 1998 Department of Defense Survey of Health-Related Behaviors among Military Personnel." Research Triangle Park, N.C.: Research Triangle Institute, April 22, 1999.

Buckley, Kevin. 1991. *Panama: The Whole Story.* New York: Simon and Schuster.

Burrowes, Reynold. 1988. *Revolution and Rescue in Grenada: An Account of the U.S.–Caribbean Invasion.* New York: Greenwood Press.

Butler, John Sibley. 1980. *Inequality in the Military: The Black Experience.* Saratoga, Calif.: Century Twenty-One Publishers.

Cannon, Lou. 1991. *President Reagan: The Role of a Lifetime.* New York: Simon and Schuster.

Carroll, James. 2002. "Bush's Bunker Presidency." *Boston Globe.* March 5.

Center for Defense Information. 1993. "Military and American Society: A Clash of Values." *Defense Monitor* 22 (8): 1–8.

CNN/*USA Today*/Gallup Polls. 2002a. June 17–19.

———. 2002b. September 2–4.

Cohen, William S. 2001. "Annual Defense Report to the President." U.S. Department of Defense. Washington, D.C.: Government Printing Office.

"Colin Powell as JCS Chairman: A Panel Discussion on American Civil-Military Relations." 1995. John M. Olin Institute Project on U.S. Post–Cold War Civil-Military Relations Working Paper no. 1. Harvard University. December.

Comptroller General of the United States. 1971. "Alcoholism among Military Personnel." Report prepared for the Subcommittee on Alcoholism and Narcotics. U.S. Senate. November.

"Confidence in Institutions." *The Gallup Poll 1995.* 70–73.

Crowe, William. 1993. *The Line of Fire: From Washington to the Gulf, the Politics and Battles of the New Military.* New York: Simon and Schuster.

Davis, James A., and Tom W. Smith. 1999. *General Social Surveys.* 1972–1998. Chicago, Ill.: National Opinion Research Center.

Deputy Assistant Secretary of Defense, Military Personnel Policy. 1999. *End of Year Update.* November.

Dickerson, Debra. 1997. "An Army-Style Prep School for Minorities." *U.S. News and World Report.* December 29. 73.

Elsthtain, Jean Bethke. 1987. *Women and War.* New York: Basic Books.

Feaver, Peter D., and Christopher Gelpi. 1999. "The Civil-Military Gap and the Use of Force," paper prepared for the Triangle Institute for Security Studies project, "Bridging the Gap: Assuring Military Effectiveness When Military Culture Diverges from Civilian Society."

Feaver, Peter, and Richard H. Kohn, eds. 2001. *Soldiers and Civilians: The Civil-Military Gap and American National Security.* Cambridge: MIT Press.

Foner, Jack. 1974. *Blacks and the Military in American History.* New York: Praeger.

Forster, Gregory. 1997. "Confronting the Crisis in Civil-Military Relations." *Washington Quarterly 20* (4): 15–33.

Franke, Linda Bird. 1997. *Ground Zero*. New York: Simon and Schuster.

Geisler, Dave. 1999. "The Education of Lt. Kopacz." *American Enterprise*. July/August. 61.

Gliboa, Eytan. 1995–1996. "The Panama Invasion Revisited: Lessons for the Use of Force in the Post–Cold War Era." *Political Science Quarterly* 110 (4). 539–62.

Goldberg, Howard. 1997. "Misconduct in the Military." Associated Press. February 28.

Goldich, Robert L. 1994. "American Society and the Military in the Post–Cold War Era." In Mark Eitelberg and Stephen L. Mehay, eds., *Marching toward the 21st Century: Military Manpower and Recruiting*. Westport, Conn.: Greenwood Press.

Graf, William. 1985. "Manning the Force: A Marketing Perspective." Strategic Studies Institute. U.S. Army War College.

Gronke, Paul. 1999. "A Preliminary Assessment of the Civilian-Military Gap on Civilian and Military Roles." Paper prepared for the Triangle Institute for Security Studies project, "Bridging the Gap: Assuring Military Effectiveness When Military Culture Diverges from Civilian Society."

Gronke, Paul, and Peter D. Feaver. 2001. "The Foundations of Institutional Trust: Reexamining Public Confidence in the U.S. Military from a Civil-Military Perspective." In Peter D. Feaver and Richard H. Kohn, eds., *Soldiers and Civilians*. Cambridge: MIT Press.

Gutman, Stephanie. 1997. "Sex and the Soldier." *New Republic*. February 24. 18–22.

Haass, Richard. 1994. *Intervention: The Use of Military Force in the Post–Cold War World*. Washington, D.C.: Carnegie Endowment for International Peace.

Hamilton, James T. 1998. *Channeling Violence: The Economic Market for Violent Television Programming*. Princeton: Princeton University Press.

Harris, Louis. 2001. "Confidence in Leadership of Nation's Institutions Slips a Little but Remains Relatively High." February 7.

Harrison, James Pinckney. 1982. *The Endless War: Vietnam's Struggle for Independence*. New York: Columbia University Press.

Hart, Gary, and William S. Lind. 1986. *America Can Win: The Case for Military Reform.* Bethesda, Md.: Alder and Alder.

Helmer, John. 1974. *Bringing the War Home: The American Soldier in Vietnam and After.* New York: Free Press.

Hendrickson, David. 1988. *Reforming Defense: The State of American Civil-Military Relations.* Baltimore: Johns Hopkins University Press.

Hendrickson, Paul. 1996. *The Living and the Dead.* New York: Alfred A. Knopf.

Hirsch, John, and Robert Oakley. 1995. *Somalia and Restore Hope: Reflections on Peacemaking and Peacekeeping.* Washington, D.C.: United States Institute of Peace.

Holm, Jeanne. 1992a. "Tailhook: A Defining Event for Reform." *Aviation Week and Space Technology* 137 (6): 11.

———. 1992b. *Women in the Military: An Unfinished Revolution.* Novato, Calif.: Presidio Press.

Holsti, Ole R. 1998–1999. "A Widening Gap between the U.S. Military and Civilian Society? Some Evidence, 1976–96." *International Security* 23 (3): 5–42.

Howe, Neil, and William Strauss. 2000. *Millennials Rising: The Next Great Generation.* New York: Vintage.

Huntington, Samuel. 1957. *The Soldier and the State: The Theory and Politics of Civil-Military Relations.* Cambridge: Belknap Press of Harvard University Press.

Huntington, Samuel, and Richard Kohn. 1994. "Exchange on Civil-Military Relations." *National Interest* 36 (Summer): 23–31.

Inglehart, Ronald. 1997. "Postmaterialist Values and the Erosion of Institutional Authority." In Joseph S. Nye Jr., Philip D. Zelikow, David C. King, eds., *Why People Don't Trust Government.* Cambridge: Harvard University Press.

———. 1999. "Postmodernization Erodes Respect for Authority, but Increases Support for Democracy." In Pippa Norris, ed., *Critical Citizens: Global Support for Democratic Governance.* Oxford: Oxford University Press.

Institute of Politics. 2002. "Attitudes toward Politics and Public Service: A National Survey of College Undergraduates." Harvard University. November.

Janowitz, Morris. 1995. *The Professional Soldier*. New York: Free Press.

Janowitz, Morris, and Charles C. Moskos. 1974. "Racial Composition in the All-Volunteer Force." *Armed Forces and Society* 1 (1): 109–32.

Johnson, Douglas, and Steven Metz. 1995. "Civil-Military Relations in the United States: The State of the Debate." *Washington Quarterly* 18 (1): 197–213.

Johnston, Lloyd D., Jerald G. Bachman, and Patrick M. O'Malley. 1998. *Monitoring the Future: A Continuing Study of American Youth*. Ann Arbor, Mich.: Interuniversity Consortium for Political and Social Research.

Kageff, Linda L., and Janice H. Laurence. 1994. "Test Score Trends and the Recruit Quality Queue." In Mark J. Eitelberg and Stephen Mehay, eds., *Marching toward the 21st Century: Military Manpower and Recruiting*. Westport, Conn.: Greenwood Press.

Kahlenberg, Richard. 1996. *The Remedy: Class, Race, and Affirmative Action*. New York: Basic Books.

Kitfield, James. 1994. "Vietnam's Legacy: A Gap Still Closing." *National Journal* 26 (June 18): 1400.

———. 1995. *Prodigal Soldiers*. New York: Simon and Schuster.

Klein, Joe. 1995. "Back to Basic: The Military Can Teach the Politicians a Few Things about Affirmative Action." *Newsweek*. April 24. 35.

Kohn, Richard. 1994. "Out of Control: The Crisis in Civil-Military Relations." *National Interest* 35 (Spring): 3–17.

Korb, Lawrence. 1996. "The Military and Social Change." John M. Olin Institute Project on U.S. Post–Cold War Civil-Military Relations Working Paper no. 5. Harvard University. August.

"Like Other Segments of Culture, Military Has Had to Come to Grips with Drug Abuse Problems." 1989. *Journal of the American Medical Association* 261 (20): 2785.

Lipset, Seymour Martin, and William Schneider. 1983. *The Confidence Gap: Business, Labor, and Government in the Public Mind*. New York: Free Press.

Locher, James R., III. 1996. "Taking Stock of Goldwater-Nichols." *Joint Force Quarterly* 13. Autumn.

Luttwak, Edward. 1994. "Washington's Biggest Scandal." *Commentary* 97 (5): 29–33.

Margerum, W. H., Jr. 1983. "Integrity: The Military Profession and Society." *Air University Review*. September–October. 78–84.

McAllister, Dawson. 1999. *Saving the Millennial Generation*. Nashville: Thomas Nelson.

McClam, Erin. 2001. "After the Terrorist Attacks, Angry Americans Talk about Enlisting in the Military." Associated Press. September 12.

McNamara, Robert. 1995. *In Retrospect*. New York: Times Books.

Miller, Laura. 1998. "Feminism and the Exclusion of Army Women from Combat." *Gender Issues* 16 (3): 33–64.

Miller, Warren E., and the National Election Studies. 1998. *American National Election Studies Cumulative Data File, 1948–1996*. Ann Arbor: University of Michigan, Center for Political Studies.

"Misconduct in the Military." 1997. AP Poll, February 21–25, 1997. *The Polling Report*. March 10.

Morganthau, Tom, et al. 1991. "The Military's New Image: The Success of Operation Desert Storm Finally Erases the Stigma of Vietnam." *Newsweek*. March 11. 50–51.

Morin, R., and Claudia Deane. 2001. "Poll: Americans' Trust in Government Grows." *Washington Post*. September 28.

Moskin, J. Robert. 1992. *The U.S. Marine Corps Story*. Boston: Little, Brown.

Moskos, Charles C. 1988. *A Call to Civic Service*. New York: Free Press.

———. 1998. "The Folly of Comparing Race and Gender in the Army." *Washington Post*. January 4.

Moskos, Charles C., and John Sibley Butler. 1996. *All That We Can Be*. New York: Basic Books.

Mueller, John. 1973. *War, Presidents, and Public Opinion*. New York: Wiley.

———. 1994. *Policy and Opinion in the Gulf War*. Chicago: University of Chicago Press.

Mullen, Robert. 1973. *Blacks in America's Wars: The Shift in Attitudes from the Revolutionary War to Vietnam*. New York: Monad Press.

National Election Studies. 1995–2000. "Trust in the Federal Government, 1958–2000." *The NES Guide to Public Opinion and Electoral Behavior*. Ann Arbor: University of Michigan, Center for Political Studies.

"The NORC Series of Confidence in Leaders of National Institutions." 1997. *Public Perspective* 8 (2): 2–10.

Nye, Joseph S., Jr., Philip D. Zelikow, David C. King, eds. 1997. *Why People Don't Trust Government.* Cambridge: Harvard University Press.

Orren, Gary. 1997. "Fall from Grace: The Public's Loss of Faith in Government." In Joseph Nye, Jr., Philip Zelikow, David King, eds., *Why People Don't Trust Government.* Cambridge: Harvard University Press.

Patros, Gabriel. 1993. *The World That Came in from the Cold War: Perspectives from East and West on the Cold War.* London: Royal Institute of International Affairs.

Powell, Colin, with Joseph Persico. 1995. *My American Journey.* New York: Random House.

"Race, Sex, and Support for Women in the Military." 1992. *Social Science Quarterly* 73 (June): 310–23.

Rainer, Thom S. 1997. *The Bridger Generation.* Nashville: Broadman and Holman.

Rayner, Richard. 1997. "The Warrior Besieged." *New York Times.* June 22.

Ricks, Thomas E. 1997a. *Making the Corps.* New York: Simon and Schuster.

———. 1997b. "The Widening Gap between Military and Society." *Atlantic Monthly.* July. 67–78.

Robb, David. 2001. "Hollywood Wars." *Brills Content.* Fall.

Ruane, Michael. 1995. "Lessons Learned from Vietnam, Defeat Changed Military Mindset." *New Orleans Times-Picayune.* April 2.

Schneider, Dorothy, and Carl Schneider. 1988. *Sound Off.* New York: Dutton.

Seelye, Katharine Q. 2002. "When Hollywood's Big Guns Come Right from the Source." *New York Times.* June 10.

Segal, David R. 1999. "The Influence of Accession and Personnel Policies on Changing Civilian and Military Opinion." Center for Research on Military Organization. University of Maryland, College Park.

Segal, David R., and Jerald G. Bachman. 1994. "Change in the All-Volunteer Force: Reflections in Youth Attitudes." In Mark J. Eitelberg and Stephen L. Mehay, eds. *Marching toward the 21st Century: Military Manpower and Recruiting.* Westport, Conn.: Greenwood Press.

Segal, David R., and John D. Blair. 1976. "Public Confidence in the U.S. Military." *Armed Forces and Society* 3: 3–11.

Segal, Mady Weschler. 1982. "The Argument for Female Combatants." In Nancy Loring Goldman, ed. *Female Soldiers: Combatants or Noncombatants?* Westport, Conn.: Greenwood Press.

———. 1993. "Women in the Armed Forces." In Ruth H. Howes and Michael R. Stevenson, eds. *Women and the Use of Military Force.* Boulder, Colo.: Lynne Rienner Publishers.

"Sex and the Service." 1997. *Newsweek* poll. In *The Polling Report.* June 16. 5.

Shultz, George. 1993. *Turmoil and Triumph: My Years as Secretary of State.* New York: Maxwell Macmillan International.

Sick, Gary. 1985. *All Fall Down: America's Tragic Encounter with Iran.* New York: Random House.

Smith, Denny. 1985. "The Roots and Future of Modern-Day Military Reform." *Air University Review.* September–October. 33.

Sobel, Richard. 1999. "The Authoritarian Reflex and Public Support for the U.S. Military: An Anomaly?" Paper presented at the 1999 annual meeting of the Midwest Political Association.

———. 2000. "Confidence in the U.S. Military: Unraveling an Anomaly." McCormick-Tribune Foundation. December 21.

———. 2001. *The Impact of Public Opinion on U.S. Foreign Policy since Vietnam.* New York: Oxford University Press.

Stevenson, Jonathan. 1993. "Hope Restored in Somalia?" *Foreign Policy* 91 (Summer): 138–54.

Strauss, William, and Neil Howe. 1991. *Generations: The History of America's Future, 1589 to 2069.* New York: Quill William Morrow.

Summers, Harry. 1982. *On Strategy: A Critical Analysis of the Vietnam War.* Novato, Calif.: Presidio Press.

Timberg, Robert. 1995. *The Nightingale's Song.* New York: Simon and Schuster.

Toomepuu, Juri. 1989. *Effects of a National Service Program on Army Recruiting.* Fort Sheridan, Ill.: Research and Studies Division, U.S. Army Command. February.

Trainor, Bernard, and Michael Gordon. 1995. *The Generals' War: The Inside Story of the Conflict in the Gulf.* Boston: Little, Brown.

Treverton, Gregory. 1986. "Deciding to Use Force in Grenada." John F. Kennedy School of Government case study.

"Trust in Institutions." 1998. Gallup Polls. July 6–9.

U.S. Army. 1982. *Executive Summary: Women in the Army Policy Review.* Washington, D.C.: Government Printing Office.

Washington Post Poll. 2001. September 25–27.

Weinberger, Caspar. 1990a. *Fighting for Peace: Seven Critical Years in the Pentagon.* New York: Warner Books.

————. 1990b. "There Is One Highly Successful Drug Program." *Forbes.* April 2. 29.

Wells, Tom. 1994. *The War Within: America's Battles over Vietnam.* Berkeley: University of California Press.

Westheider, James. 1997. *Fighting on Two Fronts: African Americans and the Vietnam War.* New York: New York University Press.

Woodward, Bob. 1991. *The Commanders.* New York: Simon and Schuster.

Zoba, Wendy Murray. 1999. *Generation 2K: What Parents and Others Need to Know about the Millennials.* Downers Grove, Ill.: InterVarsity Press, 1999.

Index

About the Authors

David C. King is associate professor of public policy at the John F. Kennedy School of Government at Harvard University. He is the author of *Turf Wars: How Congressional Committees Claim Jurisdiction*, published by the University of Chicago Press in 1997. Zachary Karabell holds a Ph.D. in history from Harvard University. He lives and writes in New York City. His most recent book, *A Visionary Nation: Four Centuries of American Dreams and What Lies Ahead*, was published by HarperCollins in 2001.